# Chain Dogs

## THE GERMAN ARMY MILITARY POLICE OF WORLD WAR II

### VOLUME II

## by Robert E. Witter

PICTORIAL HISTORIES PUBLISHING COMPANY, INC.

Missoula, Montana 59801

LIBRARY OF CONGRESS
CATALOG CARD NO. 93-87778

ISBN 1-57510-013-4

First Printing: May 1996

Cover and Layout: Lady Russ
Production Consultant: Stan Cohen

PICTORIAL HISTORIES PUBLISHING COMPANY, INC.
713 South Third Street
Missoula, Montana 59801

For POOK
Elizabeth Jane Witter

# TABLE OF CONTENTS

# PHOTOGRAPHS AND DOCUMENTS

Feldjaeger Hauptfeldwebel Thomas Haardt
Hauptfeldwebel Thomas Haardt Collection

# FOREWORD

A great amount of the most varied literature is known to exist on the World War II German Army, its uniforms and history. However, many works are incomplete or treat subject matters only superficially. The second volume of "Chain Dogs" is a most valuable supplement to the first volume and contains clearly arranged additional information on World War II Feldgendarmerie units, their employment and a listing of Feldpostnummern (German Army World War II postal service numbers). Additionally, personal accounts of several Feldgendarmen serving in World War II are also included.

I am very pleased to have been able to contribute to the realization of this book with some items from my personal militaria collection. The Feldgendarmerie, a disliked and ill-famed force, preserved an unblemished record throughout the war and not a single member of the Feldgendarmerie has ever been put before a war crimes tribunal.

The present-day military policeman is just as important in a modern army as before. Many tasks have remained the same with some new tasks being added. During the first German UN mission in Somalia one Feldjaeger platoon had also taken part. Besides the fact that the traditional name "Feldjaeger" has been preserved, we also wear the old Prussian guard star as a beret badge.

D-56070 KOBLENZ, Germany, September 1994          Thomas Haardt

Author's Note:  Master Sergeant (Hauptfeldwebel) Thomas Haardt presently serves with the 5th Company, MP Battalion 740 in Koblenz and served with the MP Platoon at BELED WEYNE, Somalia.

# INTRODUCTION

Fifty million people died as a result of the Second World War. Three hundred thousand Americans, five hundred thousand British, twenty million Soviets, four million, five hundred thousand Germans, two million Japanese, five hundred thousand Italians, and on, and on, and on. The numbers are staggering but, in our present world of big numbers - the speed of missiles gauged in miles-per-hour, the number of molecules in the human body, the circumference of the Earth, the depth of the oceans, even the top score in a video game; all those large numbers have numbed us to the point where the big picture becomes an array of statistics and, as a result, we're psychically diverted from the number 1.

One soldier died.

It doesn't matter what country's uniform he wore, or why he fought. The fact is he was born of a mother and father. He grew throughout childhood and adolescence, perhaps he had a brother or sister. He may have been the youngest sibling and the most adored, or the eldest and expected by his parents to be a role model for the other children in the family. Whether he came from the upper-crust of society, a middle-class background, an impoverished home, or no home at all, he had touched the lives of those he lived among, and now he is dead.

Hopefully, someone, somewhere, grieves for him. Is it his mother who bore him, his elder sister who cared for him, his girlfriend who pledged to him, or his wife who married him? Is it his father who held such great expectations for him, his brother who idolized him, his buddy who shared with him, or his children who loved and depended upon him? The point is, he is dead!

He was a whole, living, breathing, thinking, person. But now, to the majority of the World, he's just a number - a statistic. He was one member of an army engaged in the pursuit of killing members of another army. He may have been successful at what he did, for a time....

To a few his death is a victory, to others a source of deep anguish but, to the majority, his death is nothing more than a single digit added to the six, seven or eight digit total.

Max Mirlach was one of the many.

He was one man of four million,

Zum treuen Gedenken
an meinen innigstgeliebten Gatten,
herzensguten Sohn und Bruder

MAX MIRLACH

Obergefr.i.e.Feldgendarmerie-Trupp

geboren 18. April 1911
gefallen 31. Mai 1944 b. Brest-Li-Kowel.

Nicht wir allein, die um Dich weinen,
Nein, wer Dich kannte, liebte Dich.
Der Herr auch kennt u. liebt die Seinen
Drum nahm er früher Dich zu sich.

five hundred thousand Germans killed during the Second World War. From this pitiful death notice we know that he was a husband, brother and son; that he served in a Feldgendarmerie Trupp (German Army Military Police Troop); was born on 18 April 1911, and died on 31 May 1944, at a place called Brest-Li- Kowell. How different was he from one of the other fifty million? Certainly, not all of the fifty million were soldiers but, like them, he dreamed, loved and died. He was not a great warrior, or his death would have occasioned a greater tribute. He was not a renowned statesman for, had he been, he never would have been a simple soldier. If he died at the front, he was probably buried close to where he fell and, since his death occurred on the Eastern Front, his grave is probably neither marked nor attended. Moreover, in all likelihood, he could have been one of hundreds simply dropped in a pit shovelled out by a bulldozer.

How many remember Obergefreiter Max Mirlach or, if they do, how many will remember him twenty, thirty or forty years from now?

This book is not about Herr Mirlach, but it is about men like him who did what he did. Through personal interviews, correspondence, wartime documents and photographs I have attempted to tell the stories of four particular Feldgendarme and of the times in which they lived.

When you read about the men in this book, think of Max, and try to think of the other fifty million. If you start counting them right now, at one individual per second, it would take you approximately nineteen months just to add up all those ones'.

## ACKNOWLEDGMENTS

I would like to express my most sincere thanks to the following individuals and institutions for their help in the writing of this book: Herr Heinz Heuer (Oberleutnant der Feldgendarmerie and Knights Cross recipient), Herr Hauptfeldwebel Thomas Haardt (Serving Member of the Feldjaeger), Mr. Peter Schweinsberg (Master Sergeant, U.S. Army, Retired), Herr Bruen Meyer (Bundesarchiv/ Militaerarchiv, Freiburg), Frau Kuhl (Bundesarchiv, Koblenz), Reverend Delbert Miller, Mr. Joseph A. Wotka, Mr. Barry Smith, Lieutenant Colonel Louis Brown (U.S. Army), Major Richard Winters, Mr. Joseph Unger III, Frau Renate Rose, Herr Otto Alden, Herr Walter Huber, Mr. Paul Brown and Virginia and Elizabeth Witter. Last, but by no means least, I want to offer my very special thanks to my parents, Mr. Benjamin H. Witter and Mrs. Roberta J. Witter, for patiently reviewing this manuscript time and again, and supporting me all along the way!

Robert E. Witter

# Pre-War

The years in which three of our four subjects were born (Philipp Rensch, 1897, Albert Schweinsberg, 1900, and Erich Hering, 1904) were heady days for the young German nation, for their nation had emerged as an equal in world affairs, their Prussian-dominated military led the competition, their scientists excelled as the top professionals in their respective fields, and their standard of living was among the best in the world. Because of the sweeping domestic changes introduced by Chancellor Bismarck, the world our three fellows entered should have been one of prosperity and a spectacularly bright future.

The dark side, however, lay in Germany's contradictory efforts: her insatiable hunger for power and influence, and the system of binding international alliances she entered into in an attempt to ensure national security. This was a common enough problem of the times, for a great number of national leaders sought more control in world affairs, while, at the same time, fear of invasion compelled them to ally with those neighbors who might aid in their security. As a result, nations quickly chose sides as, for example, Great Britain did with France in their Entente Cordiale of 1904 - the year Erich Hering was born. From this aggressive/paranoid state of affairs emerged two armed and nervous camps whose fears, bravado and greed steadily eroded any pretense of peace.

War was inevitable and, in August 1914, the spark ignited. Briefly: when the Austro-Hungarian Archduke Franz Ferdinand and his wife were murdered in Bosnia by a Serbian assassin, Germany pressured Austria-Hungary to punish Serbia for the event. Russia, Serbia's ally, began preparing for war, but Germany beat her to the punch and declared war on Russia. Since France was allied to Russia, she called up her troops but, once again, Germany declared war against her first. When Germany invaded neutral Belgium on her advance into France, Great Britain (allied to Russia and France) declared war on Germany. Germany, Austria-Hungary, and their allies became known as the Central Powers, while those nations waging war against them were called the Allies. Although Italy was a member of the Central Powers, she determined that her allies were destined to lose, so she chose to switch sides in 1915 in the hopes of extracting Austrian land at war's end. After much debate and provocation, the United States entered the war on the side of the Allies in 1917. This brutal war seemed to favor the Germans until 1918, when fresh American troops entered the fighting. From that point on, the Central Powers found themselves steadily beaten back and, on 11 November 1918, an armistice ended the warfare that had claimed nearly ten million lives.

Heinz Heuer, having been born on 2 March 1918, was not yet a year old when the war ended. Philipp Rensch and Albert Schweinsberg both served in the German Army during the war - Rensch was a combatant, and Schweinsberg was just finishing his military training when the war ended. Erich Hering, fourteen years old when the Armistce was signed, missed the fighting, but could not have missed the post-war repercussions.

Eighteen year old Albert Schweinsberg, Jueterbog/Berlin, 1918.

First, and most importantly, the average German did not, facts aside, acknowledge the defeat of their army. They saw no clear cut military reverses that could not be surmounted, and their generals claimed that they had been "stabbed in the back" by their politicians for admitting defeat and accepting the terms of the armistice. To most Germans the Treaty of Versailles was an intolerable punishment that could have been averted had their military been permitted to continue the war.

Schweinsberg joined up in 1917, and was completing his training with the II. Guards Artillery Regiment at the Artillery School in Jueterbog/Berlin when the war ended.

Not having been to the front, it is very likely that Albert shared his countrymen's prevalent misconception and regretted not having had the opportunity to fight. Rensch may have had another opinion for, as a combat veteran, he was probably aware of the true situation: the German Army had suffered more than enough and, in early 1918, revolutions occurred throughout Germany in which soldiers, sailors and workers sought to end the war. The Kaiser abdicated, fled into exile, and Germany was declared a Republic. Hering, the youthful teenager, must have looked about himself, saw his Kaiser run off, his government changed, his countrymen screaming "foul" and, probably, felt the same as Schweinsberg.

Secondly, the form of government that succeeded the Monarchy - the Weimar Republic - was weak and ineffectual. The treaty they had signed with the victors was far more harsh than the Germans expected; they were incapable of combatting the internal and external forces (Communists, royal supporters and neighboring nations) that battered and attempted to split their country, and rampant inflation that

Albert Schweinsberg in Freikorps uniform. Note the skull and crossed bones device on his cap.

ruined many German families was beyond the Republic's ability to remedy.

We don't know how Rensch and Hering responded to these situations, but Albert Schweinsberg joined a Freikorps detachment in March, 1919.

The right wing, para-military Freikorps were initially a supplement for the greatly reduced (and unreliable) German army. Serving as a ready reserve, many of their members were former officers, demobilized soldiers, disgruntled citizens, and unemployed nationalists. As a member of the 4th Regiment, II. Naval Brigade "Ehrhardt" (Freikorps), Schweinsberg fought in the Battle of Annaberg in eastern Upper Silesia when the Poles attempted to annex this territory, battled the Communists in central Germany, and participated in the "Kapp Putsch" of March, 1920.

Members of the Ehrhardt Brigade in Upper Silesia, 1919.

Ehrhardt Brigade in the East, 1920.

Freikorps member Schweinsberg just before the "Kapp Putsch", 24 February 1920.

This last event, the "Kapp Putsch" was an attempt by the Freikorps to overthrow the Republic and establish a new, right wing government under Wolfgang Kapp - a journalist. The Ehrhardt Brigade of the Freikorps entered Berlin on 12 March 1920, and seized control. Kapp was named the new Chancellor, and the legal government fled. Before leaving, however, the government stridently urged the city to strike. After five days without utilities, transportation, and order, Berlin was paralyzed and Kapp was forced to resign.

Group portrait of the Ehrhardt Brigade just before their official deactivation, April 1920.

As an aside, it is interesting that the Ehrhardt Brigade was responsible for first introducing the swastika (Hakenkreuz) to German politics; the men of the Brigade had discovered this ancient good luck symbol while deployed in the Balkans and, upon learning its significance, adopted it as their own and painted it on their helmets.

Upon his demobilization from the Freikorps in May 1920, Schweinsberg joined the mounting ranks of the unemployed. Finally, in 1921, - the year Adolf Hitler became the leader of the National Socialist German Worker's Party (NSDAP) - he managed to secure a position with the Prussian Police, serving in Wilhelmshaven and on the Frisian island of Borkum.

Wachtmeister Schweinsberg (left), 1922

Polizei Wachtmeister Albert Schweinsberg, 14 January 1925.

Schweinsberg spent four years with the police as a patrolman (Wachtmeister) before quitting his job in disgust over the prevailing political climate. One must wonder what would possess an individual to resign his relatively secure civil service employment when, because of outrageous inflation, the German Mark that was worth four to the U.S. Dollar when he began his employment had been reduced to 130,000,000,000 to the Dollar when he resigned.

The answer lay in this desperate young man's belief in Hitler's NSDAP. Although a great many viewed this party with attitudes ranging from indifference to outright hatred, a sizeable number of Germans saw it as a vibrant, reform-minded organization that, according to their propaganda, guaranteed to cure many of Germany's ills. Certainly, there were odious aspects to the party (anti-semitism, for one), but for frustrated soldiers like Schweinsberg and Rensch, here was a political force with which they could identify. The party leadership were, for the most part, former military personnel, and the number-one-avowed aim of the party was to restore Germany's pre-war greatness. Placing yourself in their position, would it not be difficult to resist a charismatic orator like Adolf Hitler who, having been a highly decorated common soldier from the war and voicing their innermost thoughts, had stepped forward in Germany's hour of need?

Whether or not he was viewed as a potential savior by the Germans, his speeches were listened to and hundreds, then thousands, finally millions joined his cause. Schweinsberg must have been convnced because, in 1925, he joined the NSKK (National Socialist Motor Corps - a paramiltary motorized branch of the Nazi Party).

This led young Schweinsberg to a position with the Korps der Politischen

Albert Schweinsberg (6th from right) with members of the N.S.K.K., ca.1933.

Leiter (Leadership Corps of the NSDAP) where, like the convert he was, he preached the word of the National Socialists and actively recruited new members.

Bear in mind that the NSDAP was by no means a powerful party at this time. Back in 1923, Hitler had attempted to seize power in Bavaria by mounting a Putsch against the government and, when this failed, he found himself convicted and sent to Landsberg Prison for a couple of years. The Germans were sick and tired of the bureaucrats who had, in their eyes, mismanaged their nation for the last seven years and, turning to an old war hero to take the reins of government, they voted Field Marshall Paul von Hindenburg in as their new President in 1925. Things began looking up, for in September 1926, Germany joined the League of Nations and, through the Kellogg-Briand Pact of August, 1928, the United States, Great Britain, France, Germany, Italy and Japan promised to condemn aggressive war.

Up until this time, Germany still didn't know just how much she owed the world in reparations for the Great War. Just imagine being in debt to a creditor who won't tell you how much you owe, but keeps coming by your house to take more and more of your possessions - and there wasn't a thing you could do to stop him! Naturally, the Germans rankled at this treatment so, in June 1929, a committee headed by an American banker by the name of Young, set the terms and amount to be paid by Germany. The Young Plan was less harsh than the original terms, but it was still much more than the Germans had hoped to have to pay. Once again, Hitler stepped forward and vociferously opposed the plan and, in so doing, became a truly national figure.

By September, 1930, the German elections revealed that the NSDAP was the second largest political party in the nation. Hitler tried his bid for the presidency against Hindenburg in April, 1932, but lost. Nevertheless, by the following July, the NSDAP had become the largest party in the Reichstag and, finally, in January, 1933, Hitler became Chancellor of Germany.

What many believe was a political ruse by the NSDAP to gain more wide-sweeping power occurred on 27 February 1933: the Reichstag (Parliament building in Berlin) was set on fire and five communists were arrested, one of which was convicted and executed for the crime. Hitler pointed at this episode as an example of the lengths to which the communists would go to destroy the nation, so the on-going NSDAP program of intimidation against their opponents escalated and was backed up by the Prussian police which was led by a leading member of the NSDAP. By March, 1933, the NSDAP polled 43 percent of the vote. Furthermore, they were able to pass the Enabling Act that permitted Hitler to act without the concurrence of the German President. Seven months later, Germany left the League of Nations claiming that the other nations were not reducing their military to the level of Germany's and, three months after that, in January 1934, Germany and Poland concluded a non-aggression pact.

Meanwhile, Hitler was having some serious trouble with a branch of his party that had helped him achieve his present position. It appeared that his SA (Sturm Abteilung - Storm Troopers) was standing in the way of the support of the German Army and, under the leadership of Ernst Roehm (one of Hitler's long time friends and supporters), just might be on the verge of making their own bid for control of Germany. Whatever the true facts were, Hitler mounted a bloody purge of the SA and struck out at other opponents as well on the night of 30 June 1934. Very shortly thereafter, in August, President Hindenburg died and Hitler immediately proclaimed himself Fuehrer (Leader) and Chancellor of the German nation. Moreover, to head off any more potential problems with the Armed Forces, Hitler required all members of the German military to swear an oath of allegiance to the head of state - himself! In March, 1935, Hitler announced that henceforth the German nation would have compulsory military service.

One year later, the demilitarized Rhineland was re-occupied by German troops. France or Great Britain could still have sent the Germans packing, but all they did was verbally oppose the action. In addition to coming across as a great hero and clever politician, Hitler was viewed as an inspired military genius for, had he listened to his cautious generals, he would never have dared to retake the Rhineland. As a result, his audacity cowed the German High Command - a very serious event that would later have disastrous consequences.

Heinz Heuer, the son of a salesman, sought to join the police in 1936. In accordance with the required military service obligation prior to entering the police school, he served with two Luftwaffe Anti-Aircraft Regiments and was posted for a time in Spain with the Reich Air Ministry. At the time, Spain was in the midst of a civil war between Loyalist and Nationalist forces. What began as an internal conflict over Spanish government was, after outside assistance was sought, a testing ground between the fascists and communists: Germany and Italy backed the Nationalists and the Soviet Union backed the Loyalists. Using new weapons and tactics, Germany and the Soviet Union slugged it out on Spanish soil and spilled Spanish blood. This testing of arms continued until the Nationalist victory in 1939, when the Loyalist forces were defeated and General Franco established a dictatorship.

Meanwhile, in January, 1937, Hitler publically repudiated all of the provisions of the Treaty of Versailles. Fourteen months later, on 12 March 1938, his troops marched into Austria - without opposition - and, the next day, named Austria a territory of the Reich. The Sudeten Germans wanted the same thing for themselves, but Czechoslovakia was unwilling to cede the Sudetenland to Germany. When it appeared that armed conflict might break out, British Prime Minister Chamberlain went to Germany to see if some kind of amicable accord could be reached. Hitler made some vague promises to Chamberlain and, although France was prepared to defend Czechoslovakia, she was dissuaded by the British. The Czechs found themselves virtually abandoned by their western allies and German troops moved into the Sudetenland.

In November 1938 (the month Herr Heuer began his police training in Potsdam), the assassination of a German diplomat in Paris by a young Jewish Pole resulted in a massive retaliation by elements of the NSDAP. Rampant destruction of Jewish businesses and synagogues throughout Germany on the night of 9/10 November left the streets littered with broken glass -hence the name for this event: Kristallnacht (Crystal Night). An investigation later conducted by the NSDAP fixed the blame on the Jews, and they were required to pay 1 billion marks for the assassination of the diplomat, and 6 million marks for the destruction of Jewish property - all proceeds went to the state coffers!

In March 1939, all of Czechoslovakia was occupied by the Germans and her western part (what is now the Czech Republic) was named a Protectorate of the Reich. Too late to do much about the Czech situation, Britain and France promised Poland that they would defend her. The next month, Hitler refused to permit American President Roosevelt to mediate over the coming conflict, renounced his 1934 non-aggression pact with Poland, and demanded both the city of Danzig and a corridor linking this city, East Prussia and the rest of Germany. Two months after that, May 1939, Germany and Italy announced their alliance, known as the "Pact of Steel."

Despite all of Hitler's avowed grievances against the communists and the Soviet Union, Germany and the Soviet Union announced a non-aggression pact on 24 August 1939. What the rest of the World didn't know was that Hitler had already decided to take Poland by force and, in consonance with that decision, did not yet want to go to war with the USSR. Part of their pact involved the planned division of Poland; when Germany invaded from the west, the Soviets intended to mount their own offensive against Poland from the east.

On the night of 31 August 1939, it was reported that a German radio station in the town of Gleiwitz had been attacked by the Poles. In actuality, there never was any attack, and the dead "Polish" attackers found in the vicinity were the corpses of concentration camp inmates dressed in Polish uniforms. Hitler had his "provocation" and, the next morning, 1 September, Germany invaded Poland.

World War I, Part II, had begun.

Very early war photo of Ordnungspolizei serving as Feldgendarme. Note the civilian Opel convertible, the breeches with high-top boots, the "Sam Browne" cross straps, and the single rifle ammo pouch worn on the left side of each individual.

Very early war photo of an Ordnungspolizei Hauptwachtmeister (serving as a Feldgendarm) getting a meal from a mobile field kitchen. Note that he is wearing the Police style decal on his helmet and carries the bayonet knot.

# War Time

On the night of 31 August 1939, the Wehrmacht waited silently and anxiously along the 1,750 mile Polish border. Young panzer soldiers nervously made last minute checks of their armored vehicles; infantrymen, hunkered down and watchful, awaited the signal for attack; commanders, having planned, organized and agonized over possible scenarios for the coming campaign, watched their clocks slowly tick off the minutes before the invasion. As the first hint of morning turned the sky from indigo to deep pearl grey, the fog swirling among their positions, the clock registered 4:45 and the command to attack spread down the line. Accompanied by the harsh, ripping sound of machineguns, the throaty roar of armored vehicles, and the incessant drone of advancing aircraft, the German Army leapt from their places of concealment and swept onto Polish soil.

The Poles had a relatively large army to oppose the invaders, but their equipment was in short supply and they were by no means prepared for the surprise and speed of the German Blitzkrieg (Lightning War). Operating against an army prepared for a repetition of the ponderous tactics of the First World War, the Germans struck in three phases that left the bulk of the Polish forces shattered, confused and demoralized. First of all, the Luftwaffe (German Air Force) launched a pre-emptive aerial assault that virtually destroyed the Polish Air Force on the ground, bombed out communications centers and transportation lines, and dive- bombed Polish troops - causing panic and disrupting counter- measures. Secondly, light, motorized German units raced ahead to engage their targets while heavy armored units swept in as pockets of steel to support the lighter units. Third, the infantry - supported by artillery - brought up the rear to clear out areas of resistance and occupy conquered territory.

The offensive directed against Poland involved 53 German divisions with more than 1.5 million men and over 1,700 tanks. In a perfect maneuver (from the German standpoint), all personnel involved in the operation would know precisely where they were going, what they had to do, and how they were going to do it; but nothing is perfect, and orders from above are often challenged by unexpected situations that delay and hinder a planned operation. One means of overcoming problems is to have a representative of command on site to ensure the progress of the undertaking. An answer to this was the Feldgendarmerie (German military police). Feldgendarme had the authority to act on behalf of the senior commanders to direct military traffic, preserve discipline, and ensure compliance with the commanders' orders. Early on, aware that war could break out at any time, the German High Command hurriedly began forming units of Feldgendarme in August of 1939. Since their time was limited, they mobilized thousands of German police personnel who were apprised of their mission and the limits of their authority and responsibilities (see Volume I). As a matter of fact, their transition from civil police to military police was so rapid that many (initially) were obliged to wear all or parts of their police uniform while serving as Feldgendarme.

A Feldgendarmerie officer standing by his requisitioned civilian vehicle - a BMW 326 two-door convertible.

Feldgendarmerie vehicle (Wanderer W23 convertible) in foreground. Jena, 1940.

Philipp Rensch, veteran of the Great War, joined the German Army on 1 September 1939. Since the end of the First World War, Herr Rensch pursued a career as a police official and, upon retirement, worked as a traveling salesman.

This photograph and Page 1 comes from Philipp Rensch's Soldbuch. The picture shows him wearing the rank of Stabsfeldwebel (Sergeant Major). Of particular interest is the Bar to the Iron Cross Second Class worn on the ribbon at the center of his chest, and the Army Marksmanship Lanyard worn suspended from his right shoulder. The "Bar" was awarded to individuals who had received the Iron Cross Second Class in the First World War and had again distinguished themselves during World War II. The Army Marksmanship Lanyard was awarded for excellence in firing small arms. Page 1 reveals that he was re-inducted as a Feldwebel (Sergeant First Class), and promoted to the rank of Stabsfeldwebel on 1 February 1940.

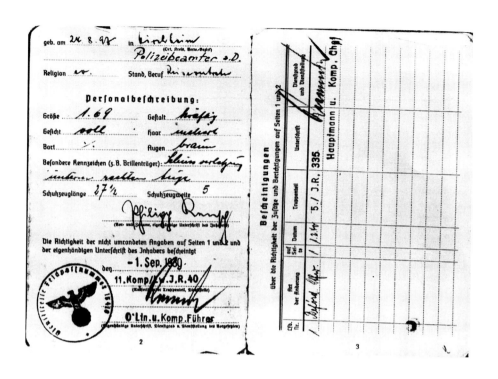

Page 2 of Rensch's Soldbuch reveals that he was born on 24 August 1897, was previously employed as a Polizei-beamter (Police Official), and a Reisevertreter (traveling salesman). His description was as follows: he had a full face, strong build, salt and pepper hair, and his eyes were brown. Under Special Characteristics it states that he had a bullet scar under his right eye. At the bottom of the page, we see that he entered the Army on 1 September 1939, and his first assignment was with the 11th Company of Landwehr (Reserve) Infantry Regiment 40.

Meanwhile, on 17 September, in accordance with the secret provisions of their non-aggression pact with Germany, the Soviets attacked Poland from the east while the Germans continued their advance westward. Before the month was out, German and Soviet troops met and Poland, with no help from abroad and hemmed in by two super powers coming from opposite sides, succumbed to the invaders.

Great Britain and France had demanded that Germany withdraw immediately from Poland back on 1 September, but after Czechoslovakia, why should Hitler have paid any attention to their demands? Two days later, 3 September, the British ultimatum to Germany expired and Great Britain declared war. Later that afternoon, the French declared war on Germany as well. Although both nations mobilized, neither committed themselves to Polish defense, but looked instead to their own borders. The French strengthened their static border fortress (the Maginot Line), while the British sent a relatively small number of troops to France. Germany strengthened her border defenses (the Siegfried Line) as well, and both sides settled in for what became known as the "Phony War" - an apparent stalemate that lasted until mid 1940.

What was not apparent to the western powers was that Germany had concentrated nearly all of her military might in the east to deal with Poland, thus leaving only a token force to defend her western borders. Germany spent the months following the conquest of Poland by consolidating her territorial gains and preparing her army for the campaign in the west.

Hitler had every intention of attacking and subjugating the western portion of the continent, but more pressing matters to the north demanded his immediate attention. To keep its war machine running, Germany desperately needed the ore supplied by Sweden. These shipments were transported to the Norwegian seaport of Narvik where they were loaded on ships and delivered to Germany. Ample evidence revealed that the British intended to cut off these shipments so, in April 1940, German troops moved north and occupied Denmark and Norway to keep her supply line open.

The following month, Germany attacked Belgium, the Netherlands and Luxembourg. These countries had hoped to remain neutral but, because of their geographical location, they barred Hitler's planned advance into France. The Netherlands and Luxembourg quickly collapsed, but British and French troops moved into Belgium and, instead of halting the German advance, they fell into a trap because the Germans had attacked through the Ardennes and nearly surrounded them. The majority of the British and French soldiers were able to escape this encirclement via the French seaport of Dunkirk but, because their sea transport was extremely limited, they had to leave nearly all of their equipment behind.

Feldgendarmen from FG Trupp 439 watching over French prisoners of war. Note that one of the Feldgendarme is holding a stick grenade in his left hand - a curious (but effective) weapon for crowd control!

Feldgendarm from FG Trupp 439 watching over prisoners of war. 1940.

Feldgendarm-Gefreiter somewhere in Holland. The Feldgendarm appears to be off duty because he is wearing neither a Ringkragen nor a weapon. Note the cuff title, but no sleeve eagle.

On the 5 June 1940, the Germans attacked France. As you no doubt recall, the French had a formidable wall of fortresses along her western border - put there specifically to keep Germany out. This border defense (the Maginot Line) had only one real weakness - it couldn't defend itself from any direction but the East! The French Command thought that any future war would be fought along the lines of the First World War so, since the First was a war of attrition in which the opposing armies wore each other down from more or less static trench lines, the French would be prepared by having an "impregnable" fortress wall already built and ready for a German onslaught. To their surprise, the Germans simply went around their wall of fortresses and drove deeply behind her lines. Once again, the Germans used their awesome Blitzkrieg tactics to confuse, destroy and terrorize the French. Seeing how the war was going for her German ally, Italy boldly stepped forward and declared war on France on 10 June.

On 22 June, the French capitulated and signed an armistice with Germany. By the terms of the armistice, Germany occupied the northern two-thirds and the

A very young Feldgendarm questioning a Frenchman on a bicycle. Who knows what might be concealed within that bundle?

Frenchman relinquishing a weapon to the Feldgendarmerie in accordance with standing regulations to disarm the local populace of a conquered nation

Two Feldgendarmerie NCOs guarding the site of a downed British bomber in St. Truiden, Belgium, in accordance with Number 42, Item C, of the Feldgendarmerie Vorschrift: "...securing shot down or forced down enemy aircraft, taking their crew prisoner and guarding the wreckage and dead."

Feldgendarme performed the same tasks in their own country as well. Here we see a traffic control check point in Berlin. The driver of the vehicle is a member of the SS, while the passenger is an Army NCO. It would appear that the two men in the car are in for trouble, for the caption to this photograph states: "A German army motor vehicle patrolman discovers a military car carrying a camouflaged' female passenger. This is strictly prohibited."

Atlantic coastline of France, while a puppet government "led" by WWI French hero Marshal Henri Petain retained the remaining portion of France.

Although a nation might capitulate, conquered peoples are never truly pacified; therefore, the Germans needed to provide security in their newly acquired territories. In addition to stationing troops in the cities and throughout the countryside, the Feldgendarmerie was often called upon to defend against acts of espionage, treason, sabotage and subversion; fight partisans; disarm and maintain surveillance over the civilian population, and work with all other police agencies (both German and occupied) to preserve order. In performing these functions, the Feldgendarmerie had the same (or greater) degree of authority as that of any other police agency.

Hitler fully expected Great Britain to sue for peace after witnessing the fall of France, but the British held on. Since the English Channel separated Great Britain from the European continent, Germany would have to mount a cross- channel invasion - something she was not prepared to do so long as the British air force was there to defend against such an attack. During the late summer/early fall of 1940, the Luftwaffe launched a massive aerial campaign against England to knock out the British threat from the skies, but to little avail. During what became known as the

Obergefreiter Schweinsberg with son, Peter (the fellow who so graciously shared the story and photos of his father for inclusion in this book). Hanover, late 1940/early 1941.

"Battle of Britain", the British managed to inflict far greater casualties against the Luftwaffe so, on 9 January 1941, Hitler ordered that the plans for the invasion be discontinued.

Shortly after the German victories over France and the Low Countries, Albert Schweinsberg entered the German Armed Forces and took his basic training in Botfeld - near Hanover. Because of his prior police experience, and his inclination to serve in a law enforcement capacity, he requested and was selected for the Feldgendarmerie. It is probably safe to assume that his preparation for service as a Felgendarm, and subsequent rapid promotion, was greatly enhanced by his civilian police training back in the early 1920s.

We don't know how much training Schweinsberg received before becoming a policeman back in 1921; however, if the following is any indication of his preparation, Schweinsberg would have made an excellent candidate for the Feldgendarmerie. According to former Feldgendarmerie Oberleutnant Heinz Heuer, prospective policemen attending the Potsdam Police School (for instance) studied the following subjects: Criminal code, general and special police powers; forestry, fishery and waterway codes; traffic codes; industrial codes; reporting duties; passport and identification duties; history; folk culture; first aid; sports; weapons training and instructional shooting; defense techniques; criminal police methodology; apprehensions; identification service; security and transport of prisoners; general training in correspondence; and everyday culture - eating, dancing, parties, uniform regulations, dealings with money; insurance, field service, animal protection; air defense; and typewriter and stenography courses (these last two categories only at the individual's request).

Provisional duty at police stations followed the first term examination. All courses were supposed to last one year with one mid-term and one final examination, in which many who failed to make the grade were weeded out. As an example, during Herr Heuer's training, of 214 candidates who started the course, only 89 remained through to the final exam. All candidates were required to serve with the active police and had been released either as NCOs, NCO candidates or Officer candidates.

These criteria applied as of 1936. However, as a result of the advances into Austria, the Sudetenland, Bohemia, Moravia, etc., the course length was shortened, but the number of classroom hours, as well as the practical training, was increased.

Later on, the majority of prospective Feldgendarme received their specialized military police training at one of two places: Litzmannstadt/Gornau (Poland), or Prague (Czechoslovakia).

The main gate at the Feldgendarmerie School in Litzmannstadt/ Gornau.

Feldgendarmen undergoing training with the Panzerfaust (anti-tank weapon) at Litzmannstadt. The man looking over his shoulder at the photographer is Heinz Heuer.

A member of the staff at Litzmannstadt.

Following his induction, Schweinsberg was assigned to the replacement center in Muehlhausen (in Alsace-Lorraine), Vichy (to perform traffic-related duties - this part of France was not yet occupied), and occupation duties in Macon, Dijon, and Bar-le-Duc.

Feldgendarm Schweinsberg at guard booth in Dijon.

Back in 1935, in an effort to enlarge her empire, Italy (under the dictatorship of Benito Mussolini) attacked Ethiopia (then called Abyssinia). Despite the fact that they opposed men armed for the most part with spears and arrows, Italy's machine-guns, tanks, aircraft and, at times, poison gas, still had a difficult time of it. Nevertheless, by May 1936, Ethiopia finally surrendered.

At about the same time Hitler tried to defeat the British Air Force, Italy attacked and overran the small British forces stationed in British Somaliland. Further on, however, their advance into Egypt met with stiff British resistance so, in early 1941, Hitler dispatched troops to North Africa to assist them.

Meanwhile, back to the east, Germany signed a treaty with Yugoslavia in March; however, when the Yugoslavian military rebelled against the treaty, Hitler ordered the country crushed. Germany attacked on 6 April, eleven days later, Yugoslavia surrendered.

The Italians, not having done so well against the British in North Africa, decided that an easier victory might lie in Greece. They attacked, but the Greeks, too, were far more than they could handle - they drove the Italians out of their country and pursued them into Albania. Once again, Hitler was forced to bail Mussolini out; his troops attacked Greece and conquered it by the end of April.

The next month, recognizing that the island of Crete could become a staging area for a British assault on Greece, Germany invaded Crete to occupy the region and defeat the British troops who had fled there from Greece. In a combined airborne and sea attack launched on 20 May, the Germans destroyed the British garrison and occupied the entire island by the end of the month. Furthermore, by Spring 1941, the German troops sent to North Africa reversed the Italian losses and drove the British back into Egypt.

Having to support (and finally take charge of) Italy's offensives in North

Feldgendarm at a desert crossroads in North Africa, June, 1941.

Africa and Greece, Hitler was forced to delay his next important offensive: the invasion of the Soviet Union. The non-aggression pact with the Soviet Union notwithstanding (it had only been a pact of convenience for Germany to deal with the west first), Hitler had two major reasons for attacking the Soviet Union. First of all, he wanted to knock the Soviets out before they could launch their own attack on Germany. The Soviets had already acted aggressively by going after areas beyond the Polish agreement - western Lithuania, the Rumanian province of Northern Bukovina, and Finland (who was an ally and major ore exporter to Germany). Secondly, Hitler was convinced that Great Britain was holding out only because she felt that the Soviet Union would intervene and draw German forces away from her. Hitler planned a three-pronged attack: the Northern part of his forces would strike out at the ports on the Baltic Sea and the city of Leningrad; the center portion would smash through Belorussia and on to the Soviet capital of Moscow; and the southern forces would drive through the Ukraine to Kiev and beyond.

The border between the German and Soviet forces stretched from the Baltic to the Black Sea, a distance of over 1,350 miles. Should Germany attack, this front

Feldgendarmerie Officer with goggles and rubberized motoring coat sitting in a camouflaged staff car within the woods. The opening phase of the attack on the Soviet Union, 1941.

would, in time, expand to over 2,000 miles in length. Moreover, such a venture would mean a two-front war - something even Hitler had railed against in his book Mein Kampf! But, despite his generals' objections, he was determined to do it and, marshalling his forces for the campaign, he assembled in excess of 3,000,000 men, 3,300 tanks, 600,000 other vehicles, 7,000 artillery pieces, 2,770 aircraft and 625,000 horses - the largest army in history ever committed to an invasion! The attack took place in the early morning hours of 22 June 1941, and the German High Command expected the operation to last no more than ten weeks!

Feldgendarmerie Traffic control in Kharkov.

Feldgendarm giving directions to a motorcyclist.

What appears to be an interrogation of an individual in which a number of Feldgendarmen are in attendance.

On 13 August 1941, a thirty-seven year old building contractor from Siegen by the name of Erich Hering entered the German Armed Forces. Whether it was his age (the Feldgendarmerie had a preponderance of older men), or his abilities, we'll never know precisely how, or why, he was selected for the role of a military police-man.

This is a photograph of Erich Hering taken from his Soldbuch, and was probably taken when he entered the Armed Forces. Of particular interest is that this photograph shows him wearing civilian clothing - most Soldbuch photographs have the owner dressed in uniform.

Page 2 of Hering's Soldbuch shows that he was born on 28 November, 1904; resided in Siegen; his religion was Evangelical; his previous profession was that of a building contractor; that he stood 184 centimeters in height, had an oval-shaped face, no facial hair, slender build, blonde hair, grey eyes, and had a scar on his head. It goes on to reveal that he entered the Armed Forces on 13 August 1941, and that the unit issuing his Soldbuch was a regional defense replacement battalion.

Whatever his initial qualifications, Hering completed his training and was promoted to Feldgendarm (the entry rank for a member of the Feldgendarmerie) on 27 November 1941, as a member of the 2nd Company, Feldgendarmerie Abteilung (mot.) 531. Given the date, we know that Hering's assignment to this unit meant that he was transferred to the central part of the Soviet Union.

This is page 3 from Hering's Soldbuch; it reflects his promotion and current assignment.

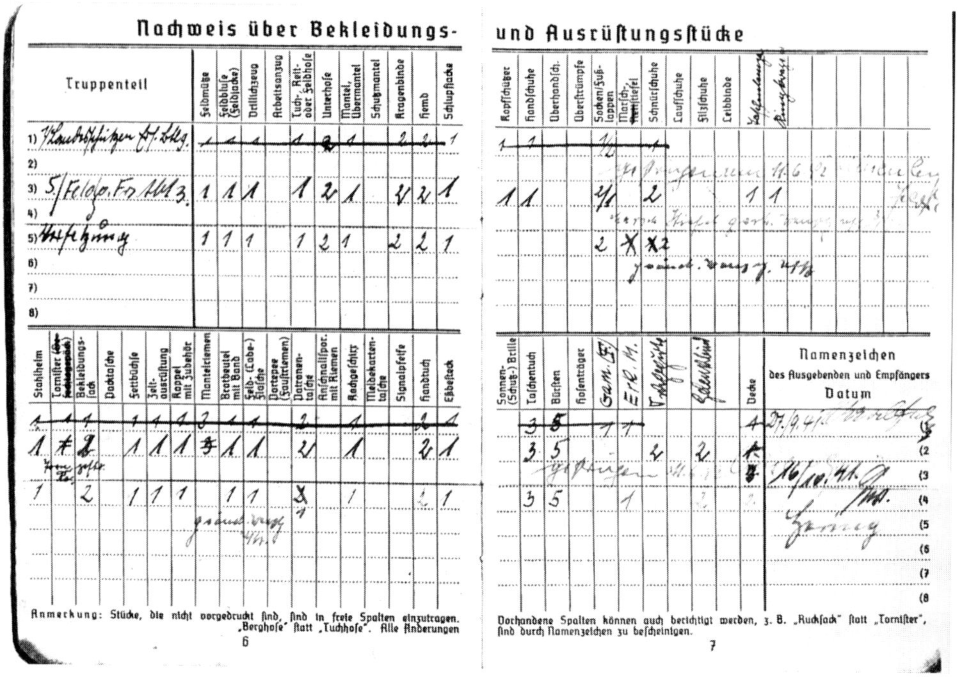

## Nachweis über Bekleidungs- und Ausrüstungsstücke

*[Handwritten entries in a two-part tabular Soldbuch form — "Nachweis über Bekleidungs- und Ausrüstungsstücke" with columns for Truppenteil and various uniform/equipment items including Feldmütze, Drillichzeug, Arbeitsanzug, Unterhose, Mantel/Übermantel, Schutzmantel, Hemd, Schlupfjacke, Kopfschützer, Handschuhe, Überhandsch., Überstrümpfe, Socken/Fußlappen, Marsch-/Knobelstiefel, Schnürschuhe, Laufschuhe, Filzschuhe, Leibbinde, etc.]*

**Page 6 entries (left section):**
1) Hauptschützen Bf. Blg.
3) S/Feldg. Er. Abt. 3.
5) Wehrmacht

**Page 6 lower section columns:** Stahlhelm, Tornister (Rucksack), Bekleidungssack, Packtasche, Seitliche, Feldausrüstung, Koppel mit Zubehör, Manteltriemen, Brotbeutel, Feld-(Lade-)tasche, Dartasche (Spaltriemen), Patronentasche, Anschnallpor. mit Riemen, Meldekartentasche, Signalpfeife, Handbuch, Elbasjack

**Page 7 columns:** Sonnen-(Schutz-)Brille, Taschentuch, Bürsten, Nasentrager, ..., Decke, Namenzeichen des Ausgebenden und Empfängers / Datum

Namenzeichen entries:
(2
(3) 16/XII.41.
(4
(5
(6
(7
(8

Anmerkung: Stücke, die nicht vorgedruckt sind, sind in freie Spalten einzutragen. „Berghose" statt „Tuchhose". Alle Änderungen
6

Vorhandene Spalten können auch berichtigt werden, z. B. „Rucksack" statt „Tornister", sind durch Namenzeichen zu bescheinigen.
7

Pages 6 and 7 from Hering's Soldbuch list all items of uniform and accessories the man was issued throughout his time in the Army. Of particular interest is the fact that he was issued his own Ringkragen (Duty Gorget) while assigned to a Feldgendarmerie replacement battalion as a simple Feldgendarm. The hand-written entry for a Ringkragen can be seen in the upper right section of the document (Page 7.).

Feldgendarm emerging from an underground bunker in the Soviet Union (note the cuff title and sleeve eagle).

32

The same month that Hering was assigned to his first duty station as a Feldgendarm, the German Army managed to surround Leningrad and, by early December, were in the outskirts of Moscow. Nearly six months before, the German General Staff predicted that the campaign would be over within ten weeks, but here their troops were, bogged down in snow and freezing - and none of their objectives reached! The weather during that first winter of 1941/42 was so brutal that sentries froze to death while manning their posts, weapons jammed solid with ice when their lubricants froze, vehicle engines had to be run periodically throughout the nights so they would not freeze up, and cases of frostbite numbered in the tens of thousands. Since the cold and snow had done what the Red Army could not, it is fairly accurate to say that Winter had saved the Soviet Union!

On 7 December 1941, Japan, one of Germany's major allies, launched an attack on the United States' military forces in Hawaii. Four days later, Hitler declared war on the United States. That same month, the Soviets launched their own offensive and pushed the Germans back nearly one hundred miles from Moscow.

Feldgendarme drawn up in formation in the snow wearing standard Wehrmacht overcoats and Ringkragen. This picture was taken in the Soviet Union on Christmas Eve, 1941.

The following Spring, the Germans regrouped and launched a massive drive to overrun the Crimea in the hope of taking the oil fields in the Caucasus. Additionally, Hitler ordered General Paulus to take and hold the city of Stalingrad with his Sixth Army.

Later that summer, the British launched a cross-channel raid on the French port of Dieppe that failed miserably because the German defenses were far too strong. The lesson learned from this raid was that any future attempt to retake the continent would have to be made on the beaches where the Germans might be less prepared to throw them back. Aside from this, the occupation in France was firmly entrenched and, except for sporadic encounters with French partisans, life for the German invader had settled down to a tedious and cautious routine. The partisans or, as Herr Schweinsberg called them, "terrorists", were native Frenchmen who used guerilla tactics to oppose the Germans. On one occasion, Herr Schweinsberg was sitting in a cafe with a friend of his who spoke French and served as a translator for the occupation authorities. Without any warning, the terrorists attacked, killed the translator, and fled before anyone could respond. All in all, though, Herr Schweinsberg stated that he actually preferred his duties in France (as opposed to going home to Germany on leave) because at home he was always in danger of being maimed or killed by the Allied bombing raids.

Portrait of Unteroffizier (Corporal) Albert Schweinsberg. This photograph, taken sometime in 1942, shows him wearing his Feldgendarmerie "Walking Out" uniform (i.e., not on duty, but dressed for going out in public). Of particular interest are the police-style sleeve eagle (discontinued in 1943), and his unbacked collar tabs.

Here we see Unteroffizier Schweinsberg patrolling a section of French roadway on his BMW motorcycle. The wrecked automobile in the background is a left-over from the Blitzkrieg in June.

Unteroffizier Schweinsberg in front of the Feldgendarmerie station in Bar-le-Duc, Feldkommandantur 590 Headquarters, 1942.

Hauptfeldwebel Schweinsberg in Macon. Hauptfeldwebel, as indicated by the double rings on his sleeves, is the equivalent of the position of First Sergeant in the American Army. By the time of this photo, due to a lack of Feldgendarm commissioned officers, Schweinsberg commanded his own Trupp - Feldgendarmerie Trupp 975.

Schweinsberg and other German NCOs by the Saone River in Macon.

Hauptfeldwebel Schweinsberg in the company of another German soldier and French civilian in Macon.

Weapons inspection being conducted by Hauptfeldwebel Schweinsberg. Of particular interest is the weapon slung over the shoulder of the man at the front of the line - a British Sten 9mm submachine gun, Mark II - very likely a weapon retrieved from an air drop intended for the French resistance.

Hauptfeldwebel Schweinsberg (left) in the company of another German NCO. Herr Schweinsberg is wearing the 1943 Einheitsfeldmuetze (standard field cap), and both men are carrying the British Sten.

Back on the Eastern Front, Hering was promoted to Gefreiter (equivalent to Lance Corporal) on 1 August 1942. According to his documents, Hering received his promotion as a member of the Feldgendarmerie unit assigned to Ortskommandantur (Garrison Headquarters) I/278 - under the authority of the Commanding General, Rear Army Area Center.

This is Page 22 from Erich Hering's Soldbuch. It shows that he received the award (abbreviated to Ostmedaille) on 4.11.42 (4 November 1942). This award was instituted by Adolf Hitler on May 26th, 1942 for those soldiers who had served in the Soviet Union during the period November 15th, 1941 to April 15th, 1942 - the first winter of the campaign. Although this is technically a campaign participation award, it was also issued to those who had suffered frostbite in the East. The soldiers nick-named this medal the "Order of Frozen Flesh."

# Decline

In the North African Theater the British regrouped and attacked on 23 October 1942 and, by early November, the Axis troops were forced to retreat toward Tunisia. Determined to bring the war to Hitler, the Allies decided to strike in North Africa, secure the Mediterranean and, as British Prime Mnister Winston Churchill put it, hit the Axis Forces in their "soft underbelly." The Allies landed along the French North African coast in early November against token Vichy French opposition. Fighting between the Allies and the Vichy French continued for a time, but the French soon gave up and switched sides. In response, a furious Hitler ordered the remainder of France occupied.

Back on the Eastern Front, Erich Hering received the Winterschlacht im Osten Medal (Winter Battle in the East) on 4 November, for his service in the Soviet Union during that first brutal winter.

Meanwhile, General Paulus and his Sixth Army were still slugging it out with the Soviet Army for possession of Stalingrad. Even though Paulus had repeatedly requested that his Army be withdrawn from what was obviously an untenable situation, Hitler refused. In the third week of November, the Soviets counterattacked and surrounded the Germans at Stalingrad within a week.

On 1 January 1943, Erich Hering was promoted to Unteroffizier (equivalent to Corporal). The next month, the last Germans in Stalingrad surrendered to the Soviets. The Sixth Army had started out with approximately 330,000 men but, by the time of their surrender, their numbers had been whittled down to under 100,000. Of those that surrendered to the Soviets, only about 5,000 ever returned to Germany - the remainder died while in captivity.

Winterschlacht im Osten, 1941-1942.

On 13 May 1943, with no hope of evacuation - much less the ability to defend - the last German and Italian troops in North Africa surrendered in Tunisia. With Africa secured, the Allies crossed the Mediterranean and invaded German-held Sicily on 10 July - at the height of one of Germany's most desperate offensives in the East. On 5 July the Germans attempted a massive armored breakthrough eastward to the Soviet city of Kursk. The Soviets had known for quite some time that the Germans intended to attack in this region, so they were well-prepared when the offensive occurred. In all, over 2,000,000 men, 6,000 tanks and 5,000 aircraft from both sides were involved in the greatest tank battle of the war. One week later, Hitler accepted the fact that the offensive was doomed and ordered the battle discontinued.

Back in Sicily, the German forces fought a delaying action and on 17 August the last remnants of their forces departed the island.

Eight days later, an Italian uprising ousted Mussolini, and their new leader - Field Marshal Badoglio - began conducting secret talks with the Allies in the hopes of securing a separate peace. On 3 September Italy formally surrendered to the Allies; nevertheless, the Germans were determined to continue the fight for every inch of Italian soil. As a matter of fact, the last of the Germans left to fight in Italy didn't surrender until 2 May 1945.

Despite his police experience, Herr Rensch did not serve in any law-enforcement capacity until his assignment to Zugwachabteilung 512 (Train Security Battalion 512) on 28 February 1943. Later, from sometime around 11 January 1944, Rensch served with the 4th Staffel (Echelon) of Zugwachabteilung 520 (Train

This was Stabsfeldwebel Rensch's Zugwach Pass. This "Temporary Document" states that Stabsfeldwebel (Sergeant Major) Rensch, of Railroad Protection Battalion 520, is performing the duties of railway security during the months of January and February, 1944. It further states that all branches of the Armed Forces, and those services attached to the Armed Forces, are to give their support to the bearer of this document in the execution of his duties.

Zugwachabteilung 52o

Berlin-Friedrichshagen, den 11.1.1944
Hahns-Mühle 12
Tel.: 64 66 89

Vorläufiger  -  A u s w e i s !

Der .Stabsfeldwebel .R.e.n.sc.h.. von der Zugwachabteilung 52o reist im Monat .Januar.und.Februar... 1944 als Zugstreife. Er hat Aufenthaltserlaubnis am Zielort.
Alle Dienststellen der Wehrmacht und der Wehrmacht unterstellten Verbände haben den Inhaber dieses Ausweises zu unterstützen und ihm jede dienstliche erforderliche Hilfe zu gewähren.

Hauptmann und stellv. Abt.-Kdr.

Security Battalion 520). Since the rail service was one of the primary sources of transportation, it was imperative that a security service monitor the passengers and determine the validity of their business. Consequently, personnel assigned to the Zugwache checked passengers' documents, identity, and, when they detected anyone breaking the law, apprehended them and turned them over to the proper authorities.

Zugwache man on a train checking papers.

After various other assignments, Rensch served with the 1st Company of Feldgendarmerie Abteilung (motorized) 541 and Feldgendarmerie Trupp 534 as a military policeman.

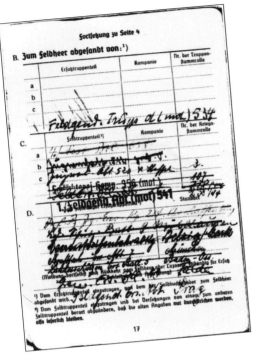

Page 17 of Rensch's Soldbuch is a list of his assignments; among which were Feldgendarmerie Battalion 541 and Feldgendarmerie Trupp 534.

Back on the Eastern Front, the Germans were retreating all along the line. No longer able to mount an offensive, their daily lives consisted of temporary halts, desperate defenses, and bloody retreats.

Feldgendarme catching a quick meal on the side of a road in the Soviet Union, 1944. Two of the three men pictured are wearing the Ringkragen, and all three are wearing the rubberized motoring coat.

On 21 May 1944, Unteroffizier Hering was involved in close combat at a town called Nowo Shitje. At this stage of the war, it was not uncommon for soldiers of all branches to become involved in combat against the Soviets, for there were no longer any "rear areas." What might have been a relatively peaceful village in the morning, could very well become the center of battle in the afternoon.

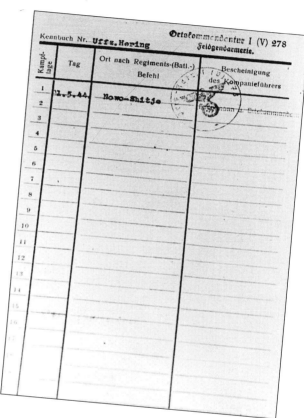

This is Hering's Kampftage (Battle Days) tally sheet. This form was retained to document the number of days an individual had served in hand-to-hand combat. Upon reaching a certain number of days, he could be eligible for awards and/or decorations.

This badge is the Nahkampfspange in Bronze (The Close Combat Clasp in Bronze). Had Hering served fourteen more days in such combat, then he would have been eligible for this award.

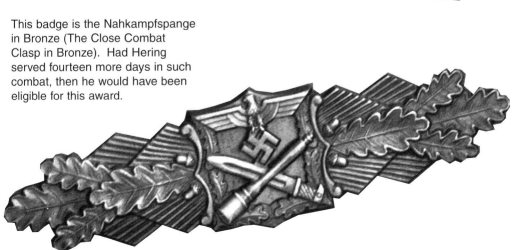

This award document states that Unteroffizier der Feldgendarmerie Herbert Scheper of Feldgendarmerie-Trupp 255 a (mot.) - 255th Infantry Division - was awarded the Infanterie=Sturmabzeichen (Infantry Assault Badge). The criteria for receiving this award was for the individual to have participated in three or more infantry assaults, counterattacks, armed reconnaissance missions, or to have engaged in hand-to-hand combat during an assault.

Infanterie=Sturmabzeichen

Feldgendarmerie NCOs and Enlisted men in formation somewhere in the Soviet Union. Note the variety of uniforms. Some are wearing the dark green collar, while others wear the field grey version. Likewise, some wear the sleeve eagle while others do not.

The same formation of Feldgendarme. It appears that these men are holding their Soldbuecher and, because there are at least two photographers in attendance, and the men are smiling, I would guess that they had just received some sort of award that was entered in their records. Speaking about Soldbuecher, since the Soviets offered a bounty for any Feldgendarm captured, it was a common practice for Feldgendarme to carry a Tarnsoldbuch (false Soldbuch) whenever the possibility of capture existed. Prior to going into a hostile area, Feldgendarme would surrender their authentic Soldbuecher at the Feldgendarmerie Direction Center and receive their Tarnsoldbuch and corresponding false Identity Disks. That way, if they were captured, their "papers" would reveal an identity other than Feldgendarm.

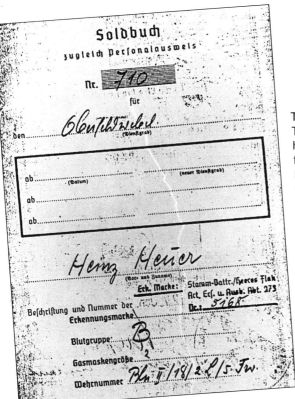

This is page 1 of Heinz Heuer's Tarnsoldbuch. It simply reflects his rank of Oberfeldwebel, and further entries throughout the book only show that he had, at one time, belonged to a Flak (Anti-aircraft) Replacement Battalion.

On 6 June 1944, the Western Allies launched their cross-channel invasion against Hitler's Fortress Europe - an invasion borne by the greatest armada history had ever witnessed. The raid at Dieppe had clearly demonstrated that any assault along the Channel coast would have to be landed on the beaches, so two likely areas stood out: The Pas de Calais, and the Normandy coastline. The Pas de Calais was closer to Great Britain (the staging point for the invasion), but the Normandy coast was less obvious and, consequently, less heavily defended. Not knowing precisely where the invasion would take place, Hitler ordered his Panzer formations to remain quite a distance inland and, when the invasion occurred, Hitler, personally, would send his armored reinforcements in to repel the attack. As a result, because of the absurd delay, only one panzer formation - the 21st Panzer Division - assisted in the first day of fighting, and even they didn't make it all the way to the coast. The invasion was a success and, by the evening of the 6th, approximately 150,000 Allied soldiers were in France. The Allies finally had their toe-hold on the continent, and the massive numbers of troops and materiel pouring in through this bridgehead spelled out the end of Germany's dreams of conquest.

Meanwhile, the French partisans who had previously mounted only small, harassing attacks, struck out with vengeance and determination. Their heightened level of operations against the Germans destroyed communication lines and facilities, disrupted troop movements by blowing bridges and railway lines, and created chaos behind the German lines.

Albert Schweinsberg and others preparing to depart on an "anti-terrorist" patrol. Two of the more interesting aspects of this photograph are the varied types of uniforms in evidence (the men wearing the camouflage are Luftwaffe personnel - probably anti-aircraft personnel on special duty), and the old French truck - a commandeered vehicle with steel plates welded to its body for additional protection. Schweinsberg complained that there was always a lack of suitable equipment and proper vehicles in France - hence, the necessity for converting the truck.

Luftwaffe Fallschirmjaeger (Air Force Paratrooper) Feldgendarm questioning a Luftwaffe enlisted man in Normandy, 1944. The old adage "a picture is worth a thousand words" is amply portrayed in this photograph. Just look at the facial expressions of the Feldgendarm and the man he's questioning!

This document is included because of the significance of the date and location of the orders. It reveals that a number of bicycles have been allotted to four different Feldgendarmerie Trupps in France. As you can see, the orders are dated 6 June 1944.

Feldgendarmen with bicycles. Of particular interest are two things: 1) all of the bikes appear to be identical so they are most likely issued (as opposed to confiscated) vehicles, and 2) all of the personnel appear to be carrying rifles. According to Herr Heuer, many Feldgendarmen were assigned bicycles - most particularly those that were stationed in big cities or towns like Minsk, Riga or Kharkov. Generally speaking, such personnel operated in two- or three-man patrols. Bicycles were either issued directly from the Quartermaster or, if stocks were depleted, confiscated from the local populace. If the bicycle was issued, then the soldier to whom the bicycle was issued was responsible for its care and maintenance - just like his responsibility for his rifle. If the bicycle was confiscated, then it was the responsibility of the Schirrmeister (Vehicle Repair Specialist). Quite often, as punishment for minor disciplinary infractions, Feldgendarmen could be assigned the task of cleaning all the bicycles belonging to the Trupp and effecting minor repairs.

In concert with the Allied invasion from the West at Normandy, the Soviets launched a broad attack from the East and, by late July, the Red Army had pushed the Germans as far west as Warsaw.

For some time now, a large number of the German High Command had been appalled with the obvious mismanagement of the war: the Allies were raining bombs on their cities, installations and factories without any real opposition; the Western Allies were back in France and also steadily moving north through Italy, while the Soviets were sweeping the German forces before them into Poland. On 20 July 1944, members of the High Command staged a coup against the regime by attempting to assassinate Adolf Hitler and secure control of the country. The attempt failed and, in the aftermath, several thousand Germans were executed for varying degrees of complicity.

By August 1944, Paris was liberated from German control and, that Fall, German troops in Greece and Yugoslavia were forced to withdraw.

This is a photograph of personnel assigned to a Feldgendarmerie detachment on the Eastern Front at a very late stage of the war. The individuals are wearing no noticeable Feldgendarmerie insignia, but the Feldgendarm standing to the left in the mid-background is wearing his Ringkragen and apparently holding a traffic wand.

Feldgendarmen from Feldgendarmerie Trupp b (mot.) 439 catching a ride on a tractor on the Eastern Front.

Hauptfeldwebel Schweinsberg (on the left) on 10 December 1944. Note that although his uniform sleeves don't bear the double rings of an Hauptfeldwebel, he carries the "reporting pouch" inside his tunic that clearly identifies him as the "First Sergeant" of his unit. Once one was appointed Hauptfeldwebel, the reporting pouch became a recognized part of his uniform.

On 16 December 1944, Hitler launched a desperate assault through the Ardennes to split the Western Allied forces and retake the port city of Antwerp. In what has become known as the "Battle of the Bulge", the Germans surprised and, in some places, broke through the Allied lines. Nevertheless, insufficient numbers of personnel, materiel and a serious deficiency in fuel for their panzers doomed the German plans. When it became clear to the German High Command that their goals were unattainable, the offensive was halted and their troops began falling back to the east. Additionally, by January 1945, the Soviets were on the Oder River - only forty miles east of Berlin.

Feldgendarm standing beside an SS NCO and guarding Soviet prisoners of war, 1945. Of particular interest is the fact that none of three German soldiers pictured is holding a weapon on the prisoners - especially considering the ratio of prisoners to guards.

On 11 January 1945, Unteroffizier Erich Hering was permitted to go on home leave. He returned to the front on 1 February and, three weeks later, he was dead!

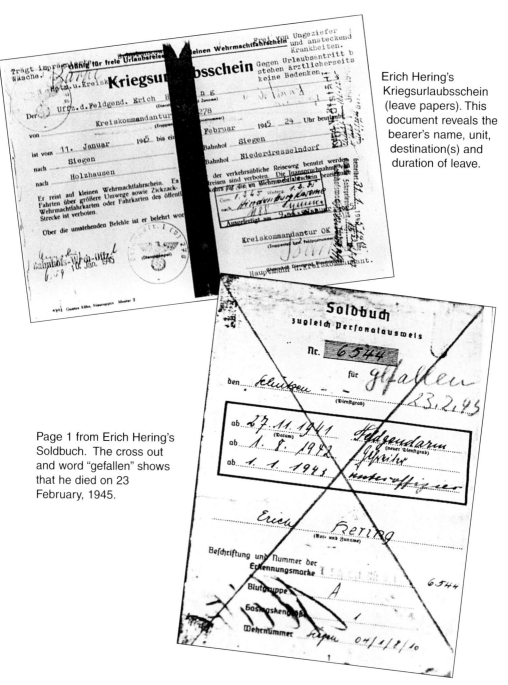

Erich Hering's Kriegsurlaubsschein (leave papers). This document reveals the bearer's name, unit, destination(s) and duration of leave.

Page 1 from Erich Hering's Soldbuch. The cross out and word "gefallen" shows that he died on 23 February, 1945.

During this same month that Hering returned from leave and died, Albert Schweinsberg was attacked by an Allied fighter/bomber while driving his motorcycle. When attacked, Herr Schweinsberg dove off of his machine and into a foxhole. The exploding bombs destroyed his motorcycle and buried him. After his rescue, and for having been buried for a time, Schweinsberg was awarded the Verwundetenabzeichen im Schwarz (Wound Badge in Black - awarded for receiving up to three wounds).

Verwundetenabzeichen
in Schwarz.

This is an order awarding the Wound Badge in Black to a Gendarmerie Hauptwachtmeister serving in the Feldgendarmerie. Something comparable to this was probably given to Herr Schweinsberg.

By early March, the Americans were along the Rhine while British and Canadian forces had pushed the Germans out of the Netherlands and were attacking Germany from the north. That April, the Soviets were in possession of Vienna - Austria's capital.

Meanwhile, during the hellish episode known as the Battle for Berlin, a period of nearly unbelievable and unremitting carnage and chaos while the Soviets sought to secure the German capital, Heinz Heuer was there as a Feldgendarmerie Oberfeldwebel.

Oberfeldwebel Heinz Heuer. Note the Gold Driver's Badge on his lower left sleeve.

Major Koessl, the commander of Heuer's unit (Cadre and Grenadier Battalion, Army Flak and Replacement Abteilung 278), had just recently divided the unit into two parts; one destined to join Army Group Schoerner, and the other detailed for a special mission to the Alpine Redoubt. At about 4 pm, 16 April, while the unit awaited departure at the railroad station in Belzig, it was suddenly attacked by Allied fighter/bombers. As a result, 80% of their materiel was destroyed, eighteen soldiers were killed, and sixty-seven sustained serious injuries that necessitated their remaining behind. During this attack, in which bombs landed every thirty to fifty paces, Heuer saved his wounded commander's life by dragging him free of the burning lead car.

Since the unit was now practically leaderless and unable to carry out its missions, Major Koessl sent Heuer to Camp Maybach in Jueterbog to await further orders for what remained of the unit. Upon arriving in Jueterbog, Heuer found that the German staff had already left and the Soviets were advancing. From there, Heuer was sent to Berlin-Wannsee where he reported to an Oberleutnant Schmidt who relieved him of his present duties and questioned Heuer about his knowledge of Berlin. Apparently satisfied with his responses, Schmidt had Heuer, a Feldwebel and an Obergefreiter taken by car to the Fuehrer Headquarters (FHQ).

Arriving at the Reichs Chancellery, Feldwebel Brueckner, Obergefreiter Sauter and Heuer were questioned extensively about their knowledge of Berlin, its surroundings, and the areas northeast and southeast of the city. After determining which area Heuer knew best, General Fegelein brought him to General Krebs. General Krebs briefed Heuer about the Soviet advance upon Berlin and said that a Soviet operational staff was located in the area of Lindenberg-Schwanebeck-Boernicke- Weesow-Seefeld-Blumenberg. Heuer's orders were these: he would command a special detachment consisting of 28 soldiers from all branches of the armed forces and, regardless of losses, he would seek out the command post, retrieve all maps and files and, if possible, avoid all fighting.

The SS led Heuer's battle group to the Jewish cemetery in Berlin-Weissensee, where Heuer found the highway already occupied by the Soviets. Seeing no other route, Heuer led his group through the fertilizer fields to Peckberge. Near Clarahoeh his group had their first contact with the enemy, so they retreated to Peckberge. Along the way, elements of other units joined them and, in the vicinity of Loehme-Weeso, the group was forced to engage the enemy in a hard and bitter battle in which Heuer's men destroyed several enemy tanks. Shortly afterward, Heuer's group discovered 40 - 50 Soviet tanks in the vicinity of Doringsee, and a Soviet supply dump in Pietzstall. While watching these areas, he noticed that there was a great deal of vehicular traffic going from these locations toward Helenenau and the Birkholzaue colony - he had found the location of the Soviet operational command post!

Heuer selected personnel from his unit who were dressed in half Soviet/half German uniforms, attired himself in like fashion and, at about 1:30 in the morning, 21 April, attacked the command post. After swiftly over-powering the sentries, Heuer's camouflaged group went on to eliminate the command post in a short battle. Maps, mail, attache cases, and all other written material were quickly gathered and taken with them. Heuer's men then destroyed the Soviet radio transmitting vehicle to cover their escape.

Because it was already impossible to return the way they had come, they moved to the Kavelberge and, along the way, knocked out 27 more Soviet tanks and almost totally destroyed the supply dump. Heuer, armed with a panzerfaust, personally destroyed 13 of the tanks, while Feldwebel Brueckner knocked out four, and Obergefreiter Sauter claimed six. The Soviets, stunned by this action and not knowing how big Heuer's force really was, were distracted long enough for the group to make good their withdrawal to the relative safety of the lake and swamps of the Birkholzaue forest.

Heuer knew that because of the number of enemy personnel in the area, his only chance to get back to the FHQ with the confiscated documents was to infiltrate the enemy lines with a few of the men and leave the rest behind. Leaving the bulk of his force with Leutnant Knackstedt to cover their retreat, Heuer and his people withdrew over the Wartenberg fertilizer fields to the Friedrichshain bunker.

At this point, he and his group were separated, and Heuer was brought before General Krebs to make his report. General Krebs studied the maps and enthusiastically congratulated Heuer on the success of his mission. As announced by Colonel General Krebs in the situation report, this operation is supposed to have delayed the Soviet advance on Berlin by three days. General Fegelein contacted his police headquarters and, on the night of 22-23 April 1945, Heinz Heuer was awarded the Knight's Cross of the Iron Cross and immediately promoted to the rank of Oberleutnant. Heuer's other decorations included the War Merit Cross II Class with Swords; the Driver's Badge in Gold (Heuer was the first police recipient of this award); both the Black and Silver Wound Badges; Thirteen Tank Destruction Badges (two gold and three black); Winter Battle 1941/42 Medal; and the Iron Cross I and II Class.

Two days later, Heuer was received by the Fuehrer and given the mission of delivering a hand-written command for General Steiner (the man whom Hitler expected to relieve Berlin) -"Come to Berlin, or else all lost!". Heuer set off on his motorcycle, but was captured by the Soviets near Hennigsdorf. Fortunately, Heuer was able to swallow both the message and his Feldgendarmerie identity sheet before he was taken into custody. Heuer was told by his Soviet captors to dig his own grave but, before the fatal bullet, a fortuitous artillery barrage interrupted the proceedings and Heuer, after dispatching his guard, was able to escape. Heuer's freedom was short-lived, for he was once again captured by the Soviets in Berlin. From there he was sent to Siberia/Tscheljabinsk and, later, to the Punishment Camp in Oms/Toms.

On 25 April the Red Army surrounded Berlin, and Hitler, who had remained there in his bomb-proof bunker, committed suicide five days later. Grand Admiral Karl Doenitz, Hitler's successor, immediately began arranging for Germany's capitulation. One week later, 7 May, Germany agreed to an unconditional surrender.

Albert Schweinsberg had retreated steadily east and, passing through the mountains in Bavaria, he ended up close to the Czechoslovakian border. When the end came, he had the choice of getting caught by the Czechs (who were slaughtering many Germans out of hand), or surrendering to the Americans (who seemed to be simply imprisoning their foe). Schweinsberg chose the Americans and ended up in a prisoner of war enclosure in Weiden. Hard rains during the month of June caused severe flooding that made the barracks within the enclosure uninhabitable. As a result, the prisoners were compelled to sleep up on the roofs of the barracks. A combination of the damp conditions and the unexpected number of prisoners caused the roofs to collapse! The American captors simply released the prisoners and told them to go home.

Philipp Rensch was taken prisoner by the French First Army and, on 10 July 1945, he served as a member of a French liaison team with the SS prisoners.

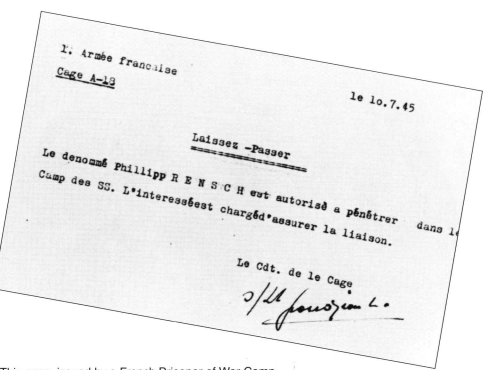

1. Armée française
Cage A-18

le 1o.7.45

Laissez -Passer
===================

Le denommé Phillipp R E N S C H est autorisé a pénétrer    dans l
Camp des SS. L'interessé est chargé d'assurer la liaison.

Le Cdt. de le Cage

This pass, issued by a French Prisoner of War Camp
Commander, states that Philipp Rensch is authorized to
enter the SS Camp in the interest of the liaison officer.

Soviet document Heuer used (under false name) to get back to Germany.

# Post War

Albert Schweinsberg, after his release from American captivity, headed to the Eastern Hartz Mountains where his family had been evacuated. This area was about to be given over to the Soviets so, in order to avoid residing under communist rule, Herr Schweinsberg and his family had to leave very quickly. Most of the other Germans in the area were unaware that the Soviets were coming but, because Herr Schweinsberg's wife worked at the registration office in the local town hall, she learned of the plans and told her family. Had the rest of the population known, there would have been a chaotic exodus. The Schweinsbergs managed to take a few of their possessions and, catching a ride on an old truck, travelled back to their native Hanover.

Once in Hanover, Herr Schweinsberg had to work for the British - cutting timber, filling in bomb craters, painting vehicles, and the like. Following this, he worked in a factory that made lampshades and, to supplement his income, dealt on the black market selling small quantities of cigarettes and coffee. Later, he became a salesman; there was no possibility of getting a job with the government because of his Nazi past.

While in Soviet captivity in Minsk, Heinz Heuer obtained the identity documents of a deceased German soldier, exchanged the dead man's photograph for his and, with the help of a Soviet female doctor (Heuer was severely ill and malnourished), was able to secure an early return to East Berlin.

No sooner had Heuer returned than he was denounced and apprehended by

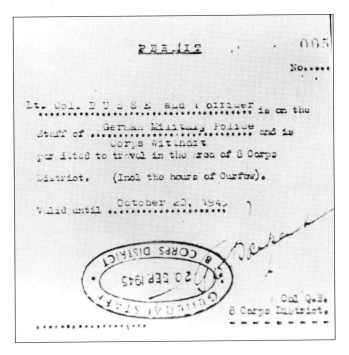

This travel permit was issued to the Feldgendarmerie Regimental Commander, Oberstleutnant Busse, by the British Occupation Forces.

the Soviet GPU in Berlin-Weissensee. Later, with the help of a Soviet officer in Potsdam, Herr Heuer just barely escaped a war crimes proceeding.

Many former Feldgendarme were put to work by the Allies doing basically the same kinds of duties they performed before the cessation of hostilities. Quite often, local military commanders simply left the Feldgendarme armed and instructed them to maintain order and assist in traffic control.

When Major Richard Winters (506th Parachute Infantry Regiment, 101st Airborne Division) was confronted with approximately 14,000 armed German soldiers in the vicinity of Zell am See, Austria, on 9 May 1945, he decided to permit all of their officers to retain their sidearms and, likewise, keep all their military policemen armed as well. "Nobody had told me, to the best of my knowledge, how to handle it. I think that I made this up on the spur of the moment. They (the Germans) worked out fine - there was no trouble between us. We weren't looking for any trouble because I only had about a battalion at that time - about 400 men probably, and we were vastly over-numbered. They could have wiped us out with the back of their hand, so you were careful about how you were talking and how you were acting because you didn't want to be ambushed here, and they could have wiped us out in a minute. The German military police were guarding their senior officers and any other duties they performed were left up to the Germans themselves. After telling them what I wanted them to do, and assigning them the areas that we wanted them to gather in and standby, I just pulled out and let them run their own show - I wasn't there to be a policeman. These guys were Prussian, professional soldiers, and I was a civilian soldier. You saw them (German military policemen) as you passed by, and they were standing in a doorway, and they were top-notch soldiers. They commanded your respect as a soldier and they were very professional. They ceased their duties after

This document was Oberstleutnant Busse's Military Police identification card.

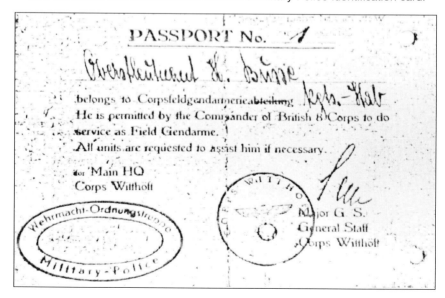

about ten days to two weeks, when all the German P.O.W.s were moved out of Austria."

According to a 1985 deposition authored by Oberst (Colonel) Heinrich Busse, the British 8th Corps in Schleswig- Holstein took this practice one step further by forming an entire Feldgendarmerie Regiment for the maintenance of discipline, military order and supporting the operations of the Demobilization Center at Meldorf.

Comprised of a Regimental Staff and 4 Abteilungen (Battalions), Feldgendarmerie-Regiment Korps Witthoeft's personnel were volunteers; the officers came from all three branches of the Wehrmacht, and many of the older officers were former members of the Police. Enlisted personnel assigned to this unit carried the Mauser 98k rifle, while officers and NCOs carried pistols. For external identification, all members wore an armband that stated: "Wehrmachtordnungstruppe" (Armed Forces Order Troops) on one line while, below, it had "Military Police". For this voluntary service, the members of the Regiment had their rations increased by an additional five percent.

Police Official
Heinz Heuer

Well, there you have it. Of our four Feldgendarme, Erich Hering perished, while Philipp Rensch, Albert Schweinsberg and Heinz Heuer survived.

I do not know whatever became of Philipp Rensch after his imprisonment by the French, but Albert Schweinsberg continued on as a moderately successful businessman and, after a long and colorful life, died at the age of 85.

After recuperating from his Soviet captivity, Heinz Heuer initially served as an advisor to the British police in Berlin and, from 1947, once again served as an active police official in West Germany.

Because of multiple serious duty-related injuries, Herr Heuer received an early retirement in 1967. After this, Herr Heuer worked as a consultant to both industry and government offices. He resides today with his lovely wife, Elisabeth, in Koblenz, Germany.

Herr Heinz Heuer

Erich Hering, Philipp Rensch, Albert Schweinsberg, Heinz Heuer and Max Mirlach are not forgotten.

# Units of the Feldgendarmerie

Several years ago, when the author first began researching the Feldgendarmerie of the Second World War, one of the many questions that came to mind was: How many Feldgendarmerie units were there, and to what units were they assigned?

Except for the extremely rare occasion when the author would come across a particular Kompanie or Trupp assigned to a particular Division, the rest remained a mystery. So many German Army Unit Histories have not bothered to mention their Feldgendarmerie units at all and, as a result, he had almost given up on ever finding a list of who served where - to be quite honest, he doubted that there even was such a list.

When the author went to Germany in March, 1994, he met with the Chief Archivist at the Bundesarchiv/Militaerarchiv, Herr Bruen Meyer. This very pleasant gentleman was waiting for him when he arrived and, after some small talk, he told him that he had assembled some information that he might like to look over. One of the things the author had waiting for him was an old, extremely over-stuffed, cardboard box containing more than eight hundred 4" X 6" cards. Each individual old, yellowed card listed a particular Feldgendarmerie unit, when it began, to whom it was assigned, and its subsequent transfers. The cards were arranged in chronological order, so the author started looking up units he knew to verify the information. Not only did the information agree, it went far beyond the facts he had learned on his own!

After consulting with his good friend LTC Brown, the author decided to compose a list, one that would benefit future researchers and anyone else interested in a particular military police unit assigned to a given unit. This list, the result of months of work at his word processor, numbers more than two thousand line entries.

To avoid confusion, the author has left all of the entries in their original German - quite often abbreviated just as he found them. The headings for each category of unit is in both German and English, and the translations for the entries can be found in the Glossary at the end of this book. This list does not cover all of the Feldgendarmerie units of World War II (for example, there are only a very few references to SS Feldgendarmerie Trupps), but it is certainly a very good start!

The list divides the units to which the Feldgendarmerie units were assigned into seven major categories: Armee (Army), Brigaden (Brigades), Divisionen (Divisions), Feldgendarmerie (Military Police), Kommando (Headquarters), Korps (Corps), Regiments and Trupps (Troops). The last category (Trupps) seems to have been non-specifically assigned Feldgendarmerie detachments that may have served as the military police version of a "fire brigade."

The following lists give 1) the unit to which a Feldgendarmerie detachment was assigned, 2) the Feldgendarmerie unit, and 3) the date (if known) that the Feldgendarmerie unit was first assigned.

Example:    1. I.D., FG Trupp (mot) 1, 18.8.39
Translation: 1st Infantry Division, Feldgendarmerie Trupp
            (motorized) 1, 18 August 1939.


Example:    Mil.Verw.i.Fr.,Mil.Verw.Bez.A, FG Trupp a (mot)
            der F.K. 723, 15.11.40
Translation: Military Administration in France, Military
            Administration Zone A, Feldgendarmerie Trupp a
            (motorized) of the Military Administration
            Headquarters 723, 15 November 1940.


Note:    The "a" after Feldgendarmerie Trupp refers to the size,  or strength, of the Trupp.  Since this was only a  projected strength, and the size of "a","b","c" or "d" changed throughout the war, the author cannot give one  all-inclusive description. Suffice it to say that a  given Trupp was a tactical group of personnel that fell  somewhere between platoon and company strength. Something else you may notice is that, in several  instances, although the parent unit and Feldgendarmerie  unit may not change, the date does. An example of this  is the 21st Panzer Division, Feldgendarmerie Trupp  (motorized) 200. The first date (4 October 1941) gives  the date that this particular Feldgendarmerie Trupp  became motorized. In May, 1943, the 21st Panzer Division (and Feldgendarmerie Trupp 200) was lost in  North Africa. When the 21st  was reconstituted in  France, Feldgendarmerie Trupp (motorized) 200 was  reformed as well; thus, the date of reformation: 15  July 1943.

Finally,  in those instances where no date was given for a  particular Feldgendarmerie unit's assignment or change, the author has  inserted a question mark.

| Assigned Unit | Feldgendarmerie Unit Designation | Effective Date |
|---|---|---|
| | **ARMEE** | |
| Armee (Army) | | |
| 4. Armee | O.K. I/623 | 18.10.39 |
| 6. Armee | FG Trupp 404 | ? |
| 12. Armee | O.K. I/562 FG | 26.8.39 |
| Oberkommando,4.Panzer Armee | Stab, 1.-3.Kp., FG Abt. 551 | 23.11.42 |
| Panzer Armee Oberkommando 1 | FG Trupp b (mot) 422 | 3.2.43 |
| Panzer Armee Afrika | FG Kp (mot) 613 | 21.2.42 |
| **Nachschubfuehrer (Chief of Supply)** | | |
| Armee Nachschubfuehrer 571 | F.K. (V)816 FG Gruppe | 2.4.41 |
| Armee Nachschubfuehrer 571 | F.K. 610/V/FG Gruppe | 2.4.41 |
| Armee Nachschubfuehrer 571 | O.K. I (V)/833 FG Gruppe | 5.4.41 |
| Uebernachschubfuehrer | FG Abt (mot) 685 (mit 1,2,3 Kp) | 21.8.39 |
| Uebernachschubfuehrer 571 | FG Abt (mot) 683 | 4.8.39 |
| **Armeeoberkommando (Army Headquarters)** | | |
| A.O.K. 1 | FG Abt (mot) 685 (mit 1,2,3 Kp) | 20.10.40 |
| A.O.K. 1 | F.K. 550 FG | 1.7.40 |
| A.O.K. 2 | O.K. I/624 FG | 17.10.39 |
| A.O.K. 2 | O.K. I/607 FG | 25.10.39 |
| A.O.K. 2 | O.K. I/641 FG | 19.5.40 |
| A.O.K. 2 | FG Abt (mot) 685 (mit 1,2,3 Kp) | 4.6.40 |
| A.O.K. 2 | O.K. I/857 FG Gruppe | 9.4.41 |
| A.O.K. 2 | O.K. I (V)/833 FG Gruppe | 11.4.41 |
| A.O.K. 2 | 4.(Ostkp.) FG Abt. 581 | 30.11.42 |
| A.O.K. 2 | 5.(Ostkp.) FG Abt. 581 | 30.11.42 |
| A.O.K. 2 | 6.(Ostkp.) FG Abt. 581 | 30.11.42 |
| A.O.K. 2 | 7.(Ostkp.) FG Abt. 581 | 30.11.42 |
| A.O.K. 2 (Kroatien) | F.K. (V)816 FG Gruppe | 15.4.41 |
| A.O.K. 2 (Kroatien) | F.K. 610/V/FG Gruppe | 15.4.41 |
| A.O.K. 4 | O.K. I/607 FG | 10.10.39 |
| A.O.K. 4 | Stab, FG Abt (mot) 697 | 15.5.41 |
| A.O.K. 4 | 1.Kp. FG Abt (mot) 697 | 15.5.41 |
| A.O.K. 4 | 2.Kp. FG Abt (mot) 697 | 15.5.41 |
| A.O.K. 4 | 3.Kp. FG Abt (mot) 697 | 15.5.41 |
| A.O.K. 6 | Stab, FG Abt (mot) 501 | 22.2.40 |
| A.O.K. 6 | 1.Kp. FG Abt (mot) 501 | 22.2.40 |
| A.O.K. 6 | 2.Kp. FG Abt (mot) 501 | 22.2.40 |
| A.O.K. 6 | 3.Kp. FG Abt (mot) 501 | 22.2.40 |
| A.O.K. 6 | O.K. I/563 FG | 30.7.40 |
| A.O.K. 7 | O.K.I/553 FG | 26.8.39 |
| A.O.K. 7 | O.K.II/667/FG | 19.12.39 |
| A.O.K. 7 | O.K. I/607 FG | 3.7.40 |
| A.O.K. 7 | FG Trupp 612 | 11.9.44 |
| A.O.K. 10 | FG Abt (mot) 683 | 12.9.39 |
| A.O.K. 11 | FG Trupp 457 | 15.2.41 |
| A.O.K. 12 | FG Abt (mot) 683 | 19.10.39 |
| A.O.K. 12 | F.K. 590/FG | 0.6.40 |
| A.O.K. 12 | 3.Kp. FG Abt (mot) 501 | 8.7.40 |
| A.O.K. 12 | O.K. I/621 FG | 9.7.40 |
| A.O.K. 12 | FG Abt (mot) 683 | 12.9.40 |
| A.O.K. 14 | O.K.II/527 FG | 2.8.39 |
| A.O.K. 14 | O.K. I/607 FG | 1.9.39 |

| | | |
|---|---|---|
| A.O.K. 16 | 3.Kp. FG Abt (mot) 561 | 25.8.39 |
| A.O.K. 16 | Stab, FG Abt (mot) 561 | 26.8.39 |
| A.O.K. 16 | 1.Kp. FG Abt (mot) 561 | 26.8.39 |
| A.O.K. 16 | 2.Kp. FG Abt (mot) 561 | 26.8.39 |
| A.O.K. 16 | O.K.II/658/FG | 19.10.39 |
| A.O.K. 17 | FG Abt (mot) 685 (mit 1,2,3 Kp) | 20.3.41 |
| A.O.K. 17 | 3.Kp. FG Abt (mot) 693 | 18.9.42 |
| A.O.K. 17 | 4.Kp. FG Abt (mot) 693 | 18.9.42 |
| A.O.K. 17 | FG Trupp d 508 | 16.9.44 |
| A.O.K. 18 | O.K. I/607 FG | 6.11.39 |
| A.O.K. Norwegen | FG Trupp 673 | 7.1.41 |
| Pz.A.O.K. 3 | Bandenjaeger-Kdo.Bischler (FG Abt 695) | 12.42 |
| Pz.A.O.K. 4 | Stab, 1.-3.Kp., FG Abt. 551 | 25.4.42 |

## BRIGADEN

**Fuehrer Grenadier Brigade (Fuehrer Infantry Brigade)**

| | | |
|---|---|---|
| Fuehrer Gr. Brigade | FG Trupp a (mot)/ Fhr.Grn.Brigade | 25.11.44 |

**Kavallerie Brigade (Cavalry Brigade)**

| | | |
|---|---|---|
| 3. Kavallerie Brigade | FG Trupp 69 | 5.5.44 |
| 4. Kavallerie Brigade | FG Trupp 70 | 25.5.44 |

**Lehrbrigade (Training Brigade)**

| | | |
|---|---|---|
| Lehrbrigade (mot) 900 | Lehrbrigade (mot) 900/FG | 16.6.41 |

**Ski-Jaeger Brigade**

| | | |
|---|---|---|
| 1. Ski.Jaeger Brigade 1 | FG Trupp (mot) 152 | 5.11.43 |

**Sturmbrigade Reichsfuehrers SS (Assault Brigade Reichsfuehrers SS)**

| | | |
|---|---|---|
| Sturmbrigade R.F.SS | FG Trupp a (mot) 778 | 22.7.43 |

## DIVISIONEN

**Fallschirmjaeger Division (Paratroop Division)**

| | | |
|---|---|---|
| 1. Fallsch.Jg.Div. | FG Trupp a (mot) 646 | 13.1.44 |
| 2. Fallsch.Jg.Div. | FG Trupp a (mot) 647 | 13.1.44 |
| 3. Fallsch.Jg.Div. | FG Trupp a (mot) 648 | 13.1.44 |
| 4. Fallsch.Jg.Div. | FG Trupp a (mot) 650 | 13.1.44 |
| 5. Fallsch.Jg.Div. | FG Trupp a (mot) 654 | 13.1.44 |
| 6. Fallsch.Jg.Div. | FG Trupp fuer 6.Fallsch.Jg.Div | 19.2.45 |

**Gebirgs Division (Mountain Division)**

| | | |
|---|---|---|
| 1. Geb.Div. | FG Trupp 54 | 25.8.39 |
| 2. Geb.Div. | FG Trupp (mot) 67 | 17.2.39 |
| 3. Geb.Div. | FG Trupp a (mot) 68 | 26.8.39 |
| 4. Geb.Div. | FG Trupp a (mot) 94 | 30.10.40 |
| 6. Geb.Div. | FG Trupp 310 | 10.6.40 |
| 6. Geb.Div. | FG Trupp 91 | 24.9.40 |
| 7. Geb.Div. | FG Trupp (mot) 99 | 15.11.41 |

**Grenadier Division (Infantry Division)**

| | | |
|---|---|---|
| 19. Gr.Div. | FG Trupp 119 | 8.8.44 |
| 36. Gr.Div. | FG Trupp 36 | 3.8.44 |
| 78. Gr.Div | FG Trupp c (tmot) fuer 78. Gr.Div. | 21.7.44 |
| 78. Gr.Div. | FG Trupp c (tmot) 543 | 15.7.44 |
| 78. Gr.Div. | FG Trupp c (tmot) 78 | 22.7.44 |
| 541. Gr.Div. | FG Trupp c 1541 | 8.7.44 |
| 542. Gr.Div. | FG Trupp 1542 | 8.7.44 |
| 543. Gr.Div. | FG Trupp c 1543 | 10.7.44 |

| | | |
|---|---|---|
| 544. Gr.Div. | FG Trupp 1544 | 10.7.44 |
| 545. Gr.Div. | FG Trupp 1545 | 10.7.44 |
| 546. Gr.Div. | FG Trupp 1546 | 11.7.44 |
| 547. Gr.Div. | FG Trupp c 1547 | 11.7.44 |
| 548. Gr.Div. | FG Trupp c 1548 | 11.7.44 |
| 549. Gr.Div. | FG Trupp c 1549 | 11.7.44 |
| 550. Gr.Div. | FG Trupp c 1550 | 11.7.44 |
| 51. Gr.Div. | FG Trupp c 1551 | 11.7.44 |
| 552. Gr.Div. | FG Trupp c 1552 | 11.7.44 |
| 553. Gr.Div. | FG Trupp c 1553 | 11.7.44 |
| 553. Gr.Div. | FG Trupp c (tmot) 553 | 3.8.44 |
| 558. Gr.Div. | FG Trupp c 1558 | 11.7.44 |
| 559. Gr.Div. | FG Trupp c 1559 | 11.7.44 |
| 561. Gr.Div. | FG Trupp c 1561 | 27.7.44 |
| 562. Gr.Div. | FG Trupp c 1562 | 27.7.44 |
| Gr.Lehr.Div. | FG Trupp 1563 | 3.8.44 |

**Infanterie Division (Infantry Division)**

| | | |
|---|---|---|
| 1. I.D. | FG Trupp (mot) 1 | 18.8.39 |
| 1. I.D. | FG Trupp (mot) 1 | 1.4.40 |
| 1. I.D. | FG Trupp a (mot) 1 | 15.5.41 |
| 2. I.D. (mot) | FG Trupp b (mot) 2 | 20.8.39 |
| 3. I.D. | FG Trupp a (mot) 3 | 2.8.39 |
| 3. I.D. (mot) | FG Trupp b (mot) 3 | 27.10.40 |
| 3. I.D. (mot) | FG Trupp b (mot) 3 | 11.2.43 |
| 3. I.D. (mot) | FG Trupp a (mot) 386 | 1.3.43 |
| 3. I.D. (mot) | FG Trupp b (mot) 386 | 1.3.43 |
| 4. I.D. | FG Trupp a (mot) 4 | 1.8.39 |
| 6. I.D. | FG Trupp a (mot) 6 | ? |
| 6. I.D. | FG Trupp a (mot) 6 | 26.8.39 |
| 7. I.D. (Stab) | FG Trupp (mot) 7 | 1.8.39 |
| 8. I.D. | FG Trupp 8 | 5.8.39 |
| 8. I.D. | FG Trupp 8 | 22.11.40 |
| 9. I.D. | FG Trupp a (mot) 9 | 26.8.39 |
| 10. I.D. | FG Trupp (mot) 10 | 26.8.39 |
| 10. I.D. (mot) | FG Trupp (mot) 10 | 15.11.40 |
| 11. I.D. | FG Trupp (mot) 11 | 16.8.39 |
| 12. I.D. | FG Trupp c 12 | 3.8.44 |
| 12. I.D. (Stab) | FG Trupp 12 | 27.7.39 |
| 13. I.D. (mot) | FG Trupp b (mot) 13 | 19.8.39 |
| 14. I.D. | FG Trupp a (mot) 14 | 2.8.39 |
| 14. I.D. | FG Trupp a (mot) 14 | 1.4.40 |
| 14. I.D. (mot) | FG Trupp b (mot) 14 | 15.10.40 |
| 14. I.D. (mot) | FG Trupp b (mot) 14 | 1.12.40 |
| 15. I.D. | FG Trupp a (mot) 15 | 25.8.39 |
| 15. I.D. | FG Trupp a (mot) 15 | 4.10.44 |
| 16. I.D. | FG Trupp 16 | 26.8.39 |
| 16. I.D. | FG Trupp (mot) 66 | 6.8.40 |
| 16. I.D. | FG Trupp 1316 | 4.8.44 |
| 17. I.D. | FG Trupp (mot) 17 | 26.8.39 |
| 17. I.D. | FG Trupp (mot) 17 | 13.3.40 |
| 18. I.D. | FG Trupp (mot) 18 | 25.8.39 |
| 18. I.D. | FG Trupp a (mot) 18 | 1.4.40 |
| 19. I.D. | FG Trupp a (mot) 19 | 26.8.39 |
| 20. I.D. (mot) | FG Trupp b (mot) 20 | 19.8.39 |

| | | |
|---|---|---|
| 20. I.D. (mot) | FG Trupp b (mot) 20 | 1.4.40 |
| 21. I.D. | FG Trupp a (mot) 21 | 17.8.39 |
| 22. I.D. | FG Trupp (mot) 22 | 18.8.39 |
| 23. I.D. | FG Trupp 23 | ? |
| 23. I.D. | FG Trupp a (mot) 23 | 26.8.39 |
| 24. I.D. | FG Trupp (mot) 24 | 21.8.39 |
| 25. I.D. | FG Trupp a (mot) 25 | 25.8.39 |
| 25. I.D. (mot) | FG Trupp b (mot) 25 | 15.11.40 |
| 26. I.D. | FG Trupp der 26. Div. | 26.8.39 |
| 27. I.D. | FG Trupp a (mot) 27 | 26.8.39 |
| 29. I.D. (mot) | FG Trupp b (mot) 29 | 19.8.39 |
| 29. I.D. (mot) | FG Trupp a (mot) 345 | 11.2.43 |
| 29. I.D. (mot) | FG Trupp b (mot) 29 | 1.3.43 |
| 30. I.D. | FG Trupp 30 | 26.8.39 |
| 31. I.D. | FG Trupp a (mot) 31 | 25.8.39 |
| 33. I.D. | FG Trupp (mot) 33 | 25.8.39 |
| 34. I.D. | FG Trupp 34 | 26.8.39 |
| 35. I.D. | FG Trupp a1 (mot) 35 | 26.8.39 |
| 36. I.D. | FG Trupp a (mot) 36 | 26.8.39 |
| 36. I.D. (mot) | FG Trupp b (mot) 36 | 11.11.40 |
| 38. I.D. | FG Trupp 138 | 9.7.42 |
| 39. I.D. | FG Trupp 139 | 9.7.42 |
| 44. I.D. | FG Trupp (mot) 44 | 24.8.39 |
| 44. I.D. | FG Trupp 44 | 24.8.39 |
| 44.I.D. | FG Trupp 44 | 17.2.43 |
| 45. I.D. | FG Trupp (mot) 45 | 26.8.39 |
| 45. I.D. | FG Trupp a (mot) 100 | 29.6.43 |
| 46. I.D. | FG Trupp 46 | 25.8.39 |
| 47. I.D. | FG Trupp c (tmot) 147 | 1.2.44 |
| 48. I.D. | FG Trupp 148 | 21.12.43 |
| 49. I.D. | FG Trupp c 149 | 1.2.44 |
| 50. I.D. | FG Trupp a (mot) 312 | 26.8.39 |
| 50. I.D. | FG Trupp a (mot) 150 | 1.4.40 |
| 50. I.D. | FG Trupp c (tmot) 150 | 5.12.44 |
| 52. I.D. | FG Trupp (mot) 152 | 26.8.39 |
| 56. I.D. | FG Trupp a (mot) 156 | 26.8.39 |
| 57. I.D. | FG Trupp (mot) 157 | 26.8.39 |
| 58. I.D. | FG Trupp a (mot) 158 | 26.8.39 |
| 59. I.D. | FG Trupp 159 | 26.6.44 |
| 60. I.D. | FG Trupp a (mot) 160 | 15.10.39 |
| 60. I.D. (mot) | FG Trupp b (mot) 160 | 14.8.40 |
| 60. I.D. (mot) | FG Trupp b (mot) 160 | 17.2.43 |
| 61. I.D. | FG Trupp (mot) 161 | 16.8.39 |
| 62. I.D. | FG Trupp (mot) 162 | 26.8.39 |
| 64. I.D. | FG Trupp 164 | 26.6.44 |
| 65. I.D. | FG Trupp a (mot) 165 | 9.7.42 |
| 68. I.D. | FG Trupp a (mot) 168 | 26.8.39 |
| 69. I.D. | FG Trupp (mot) 169 | 26.8.39 |
| 70. I.D. | FG Trupp 170 | 26.4.44 |
| 71. I.D. | FG Trupp 171 | 29.8.39 |
| 72. I.D. | FG Trupp a (mot) 315 | 26.9.39 |
| 72. I.D. | FG Trupp a (mot) 172 | 15.9.40 |
| 73. I.D. | FG Trupp (mot) 173 | 26.8.39 |
| 75. I.D. | FG Trupp 175 | 27.9.39 |

| | | |
|---|---|---|
| 76. I.D. | FG Trupp a (mot) 176 | 27.8.39 |
| 76. I.D. | FG Trupp a (mot) 176 | 17.2.43 |
| 77. I.D. | FG Trupp 177 | 21.1.44 |
| 78. I.D. | FG Trupp (mot) 178 | 29.8.39 |
| 79. I.D. | FG Trupp 140 | 28.8.39 |
| 79. I.D. | FG Trupp 140 | 15.3.43 |
| 79. I.D. | FG Trupp (mot) 179 | 11.5.43 |
| 81. I.D. | FG Trupp 181 | ? |
| 82. I.D. | FG Trupp a (mot) 182 | 15.12.39 |
| 82. I.D. | FG Trupp a (mot) 182 | 15.4.41 |
| 83. I.D. | FG Trupp a (mot) 183 | 16.12.39 |
| 83. I.D. | FG Trupp a 183 | 9.1.42 |
| 84. I.D. | FG Trupp c (tmot) 184 | 21.1.44 |
| 85. I.D. | FG Trupp c (tmot) 185 | 21.1.44 |
| 86. I.D. | FG Trupp (mot) 186 | 26.8.39 |
| 86. I.D. | FG Trupp a (mot) 236 | 10.3.42 |
| 87. I.D. | FG Trupp a (mot) 187 | 26.8.39 |
| 88. I.D. | FG Trupp a 188 | 10.12.39 |
| 88. I.D. | FG Trupp a (mot) 188 | 1.8.41 |
| 88. I.D. | FG Trupp 188 | 28.3.44 |
| 89. I.D. | FG Trupp c (tmot) 189 | 21.1.44 |
| 91. I.D. | FG Trupp c (tmot) 191 | 21.1.44 |
| 92. I.D. | FG Trupp c (tmot) 192 | 21.1.44 |
| 93. I.D. | FG Trupp (mot) 193 | 24.9.39 |
| 95. I.D. | FG Trupp (mot) 195 | 25.9.39 |
| 95. I.D. | FG Trupp c (tmot) 195 | 5.9.44 |
| 95. I.D. | FG Trupp c (tmot) 195 | 22.9.44 |
| 96. I.D. | FG Trupp (mot) 196 | 26.9.39 |
| 98. I.D. | FG Trupp (mot) 198 | 22.9.39 |
| 102. I.D. | FG Trupp a (mot) 102 | 1.2.41 |
| 106. I.D. | FG Trupp a (mot) 106 | 1.2.41 |
| 111. I.D. | FG Trupp a (mot) 111 | 22.11.40 |
| 112. I.D. | FG Trupp der 112. I.D. | 1.2.41 |
| 113. I.D. | FG Trupp (mot) 113 | 10.12.40 |
| 113. I.D. | FG Trupp (mot) 113 | 17.2.43 |
| 113. I.D. | FG Trupp c (mot) 271 | 17.11.43 |
| 121. I.D. | FG Trupp (mot) 121 | 8.10.40 |
| 122. I.D. | FG Trupp 122 | 9.10.40 |
| 126. I.D. | FG Trupp 126 | 2.10.40 |
| 129. I.D. | FG Trupp 129 | ? |
| 131. I.D. | FG Trupp 131 | 15.10.40 |
| 132. I.D. | FG Trupp 132 | 30.9.40 |
| 134. I.D. | FG Trupp (mot) 134 | 15.10.40 |
| 137. I.D. | FG Trupp (mot) 137 | 4.10.40 |
| 137. I.D. | FG Trupp 487 | 14.12.43 |
| 159. I.D. | FG Trupp 1059 | 15.10.44 |
| 161. I.D. | FG Trupp 241 | 15.1.40 |
| 162. I.D. | FG Trupp a (mot) 236 | 12.1.40 |
| 162. I.D. (Turk.) | FG Trupp 236 | 15.1.40 |
| 162. I.D. (Turk.) | FG Kp. (mot) 236 | 21.5.43 |
| 163. I.D. | FG Trupp c (mot) 234 | 11.1.40 |
| 163. I.D. | FG Trupp (mot) 463 | 25.4.40 |
| 164. I.D. | FG Trupp c (tmot) 220 | 20.1.40 |
| 164. I.D. | FG Kp (mot) 220 | 15.12.41 |

| | | |
|---|---|---|
| 167. I.D. | FG Trupp c (mot) 238 | 15.1.40 |
| 168. I.D. | FG Trupp a (mot) 248 | 15.1.40 |
| 169. I.D. | FG Trupp (tmot) 230 | 11.1.40 |
| 169. I.D. | FG Trupp a (mot) 230 | 1.2.41 |
| 170. I.D. | FG Trupp 240 | 9.1.40 |
| 181. I.D. | FG Trupp c (mot) 222 | 15.1.40 |
| 181. I.D. | FG Trupp (mot) 463 | 6.6.40 |
| 181. I.D. | FG Trupp a (mot) 222 | 23.9.41 |
| 183. I.D. | FG Trupp c (tmot) 219 | 10.1.40 |
| 183. I.D. | FG Trupp a (mot) 219 | 1.2.41 |
| 189. I.D. | FG Trupp 1089 | 15.10.44 |
| 196. I.D. | FG Trupp 233 | 11.1.40 |
| 196. I.D. | FG Trupp (mot) 463 | 16.5.40 |
| 197. I.D. | FG Trupp (tmot) 229 | 15.1.40 |
| 197. I.D. | FG Trupp a (mot) 229 | 1.6.41 |
| 198. I.D. | FG Trupp 235 | 15.1.40 |
| 199. I.D. | FG Trupp (mot) 199 | 1.11.39 |
| 199. I.D. | FG Trupp (mot) 571 | 1.11.40 |
| 199. I.D. | FG Trupp z.b.V. 71 | 10.42 |
| 203. I.D. | FG Trupp c (mot) 203 | 21.10.44 |
| 205. I.D. | FG Trupp (mot) 205 | 1.1.40 |
| 205. I.D. | O.K. I/621 FG | 1.1.40 |
| 205. I.D. | FG Trupp 205 | 24.5.41 |
| 206. I.D. | FG Trupp 206 | 17.8.39 |
| 206. I.D. | O.K. I/501 FG | 21.11.39 |
| 207. I.D. | FG Trupp 207 | 26.8.39 |
| 208. I.D. | FG Trupp a (mot) 208 | 26.8.39 |
| 208. I.D. | FG Trupp 208 | 26.8.39 |
| 208. I.D. | O.K. I/533 FG | 14.10.39 |
| 211. I.D. | FG Trupp 211 | 26.8.39 |
| 211. I.D. | FG Trupp a (mot) 211 | 26.8.39 |
| 212. I.D. | FG Trupp a (mot) 212 | 20.8.39 |
| 213. I.D. | FG Trupp (mot) 213 | 26.8.39 |
| 214. I.D. | FG Trupp (mot) 214 | 27.8.39 |
| 215. I.D. | FG Trupp a (mot) 215 | 29.8.39 |
| 215. I.D. | FG Trupp (mot) 215 | 30.8.39 |
| 215. I.D. | FG Trupp 215 | 8.11.41 |
| 216. I.D. | FG Trupp (mot) 216 | 28.8.39 |
| 217. I.D. | FG Trupp 217 | 17.8.39 |
| 218. I.D. | FG Trupp a (mot) 218 | 26.8.39 |
| 221. I.D. | FG Trupp a (mot) 221 | 26.8.39 |
| 223. I.D. | FG Trupp a (mot) 223 | 26.8.39 |
| 225. I.D. | FG Trupp a (mot) 225 | 26.8.39 |
| 226. I.D. | FG Trupp 226 | 26.6.44 |
| 227. I.D. | FG Trupp (mot) 227 | 26.8.39 |
| 228. I.D. | FG Trupp 228 | 17.8.39 |
| 230. I.D. | FG Trupp z.b.V. 71 | 10.42 |
| 231. I.D. | FG Trupp a (mot) 231 | 26.8.39 |
| 232. I.D. | FG Trupp 232 | 26.6.44 |
| 237. I.D. | FG Trupp 237 | 26.6.44 |
| 239. I.D. | FG Trupp 239 | 26.8.39 |
| 242. I.D. | FG Trupp c 242 | 9.7.43 |
| 243. I.D. | FG Trupp c 243 | 9.7.43 |
| 244. I.D. | FG Trupp c 244 | 8.9.43 |

| | | |
|---|---|---|
| 244. I.D. | FG Trupp der 244. I.D. | 6.12.43 |
| 245. I.D. | FG Trupp c 245 | 8.9.43 |
| 246. I.D. | FG Trupp a (mot) 246 | 26.8.39 |
| 246. I.D. | FG Trupp a (mot) 246 | 1.6.41 |
| 250. I.D. (Span.Div) | FG Trupp a (mot) 250 | 20.7.41 |
| 251. I.D. | FG Trupp a (mot) 251 | 26.8.39 |
| 252. I.D. | FG Trupp (mot) 252 | 30.8.39 |
| 253. I.D. | FG Trupp (mot) 253 | 26.8.39 |
| 254. I.D. | FG Trupp (mot) 254 | 26.8.39 |
| 255. I.D. | Ordnungsdienst der 255.I.D. | 26.8.39 |
| 255. I.D. | FG Trupp a (mot) 255 | 1.4.40 |
| 256. I.D. | FG Trupp a (mot) 256 | 26.8.39 |
| 257. I.D. | FG Trupp a (mot) 257 | 26.8.39 |
| 258. I.D. | FG Trupp a (mot) 258 | 26.8.39 |
| 260. I.D. | FG Trupp 260 | 28.8.39 |
| 260. I.D. | O.K. I/622 | 27.10.39 |
| 262. I.D. | FG Trupp (mot) 262 | 26.8.39 |
| 262. I.D. | FG Trupp 262 | 26.8.39 |
| 263. I.D. | FG Trupp a (mot) 263 | 28.8.39 |
| 264. I.D. | FG Trupp c (tmot) 264 | 19.5.43 |
| 265. I.D. | FG Trupp c (tmot) 265 | 20.5.43 |
| 266. I.D. | FG Trupp c (tmot) 266 | 20.5.43 |
| 267. I.D. | FG Trupp 267 | 28.8.39 |
| 268. I.D. | FG Trupp a (mot) 268 | 26.8.39 |
| 270. I.D. | FG Trupp z.b.V. 71 | 10.42 |
| 271. I.D. | FG Trupp c (mot) 271 | 17.11.43 |
| 272. I.D. | FG Trupp 272 | 17.11.43 |
| 274. I.D. | FG Trupp c (tmot) 274 | 26.5.43 |
| 275. I.D. | FG Trupp 275 | 2.12.43 |
| 276. I.D. | FG Trupp 276 | 1.44 |
| 276. I.D. | FG Trupp 276 | 28.3.44 |
| 277. I.D. | FG Trupp 277 | 28.3.44 |
| 278. I.D. | FG Trupp 278 | 20.12.43 |
| 278. I.D. | FG Trupp 278 | 5.1.44 |
| 281. I.D. | FG Trupp c (tmot) 281 | 11.11.44 |
| 286. I.D. | FG Trupp 286 | 17.12.44 |
| 290. I.D. | FG Trupp der 290.Div. | 6.2.40 |
| 291. I.D. | FG Trupp 291 | 8.11.40 |
| 292. I.D. | FG Trupp (tmot) 292 | 1.3.40 |
| 293. I.D. | FG Trupp 293 | 15.2.40 |
| 294. I.D. | FG Trupp 294 | 23.2.40 |
| 294. I.D. | FG Trupp a (mot) 294 | 13.7.43 |
| 295. I.D. | FG Trupp 295 | 15.2.40 |
| 296. I.D. | FG Trupp 296 | 13.2.40 |
| 297. I.D. | FG Trupp 297 | 13.2.40 |
| 298. I.D. | FG Trupp 298 | 15.2.40 |
| 299. I.D. | FG Trupp 299 | 16.2.40 |
| 302. I.D. | FG Trupp c (tmot) 302 | 8.8.42 |
| 302. I.D. | FG Trupp c (tmot) 617 | 28.8.42 |
| 304. I.D. | FG Trupp c (mot) 304 | 7.8.42 |
| 305. I.D. | FG Trupp 305 | 30.7.41 |
| 306. I.D. | FG Trupp c (mot) 306 | 21.8.42 |
| 311. I.D. | FG Trupp 161 | 16.8.39 |
| 311. I.D. | FG Trupp 511 | 6.10.39 |

| | | |
|---|---|---|
| 311. I.D. | FG Trupp (mot) 341 | 8.3.40 |
| 320. I.D. | FG Trupp c (mot) 320 | 21.8.42 |
| 321. I.D. | FG Trupp c (mot) 321 | 7.8.42 |
| 323. I.D. | FG Trupp 323 | 28.3.44 |
| 326. I.D. | FG Trupp 326 | 11.11.42 |
| 327. I.D. | FG Trupp c (tmot) 327 | 28.7.42 |
| 327. I.D. | FG Trupp c (tmot) 327 | 3.2.44 |
| 328. I.D. | FG Trupp 306 | 28.3.44 |
| 329. I.D. | FG Trupp a (mot) 329 | 19.5.42 |
| 329. I.D. | FG Trupp a (mot) 900 | 26.7.42 |
| 330. I.D. | FG Trupp 330 | 21.6.42 |
| 331. I.D. | FG Trupp c (tmot) 331 | 19.6.42 |
| 331. I.D. (Stab) z.b.V. | FG Trupp c (tmot) 331 | 13.11.44 |
| 332. I.D. | FG Trupp c (tmot) 332 | 21.8.42 |
| 332. I.D. | FG Trupp a (mot) 332 | 1.11.42 |
| 333. I.D. | FG Trupp a (mot) 333 | ?.41 |
| 333. I.D. | FG Trupp c (mot) 333 | 20.7.42 |
| 334. I.D. | FG Trupp (tmot) 334 | 25.11.42 |
| 334. I.D. | FG Trupp a (mot) 334 | 26.5.43 |
| 335. I.D. | FG Trupp der 335 I.D. | 1.9.41 |
| 335. I.D. | FG Trupp c (mot) 335 | 20.7.42 |
| 335. I.D. | FG Trupp a (mot) | 1.12.42 |
| 336. I.D. | FG Trupp der 336. I.D. | 12.3.41 |
| 337. I.D. | FG Trupp c (mot) 337 | 23.9.42 |
| 337. I.D. | FG Trupp a (mot) 337 | 10.7.43 |
| 338. I.D. | FG Trupp c (mot) 338 | 9.11.42 |
| 339. I.D. | FG Trupp 339 | ? |
| 340. I.D. | FG Trupp 340 | ? |
| 342. I.D. | FG Trupp c (tmot) 342 | 16.8.41 |
| 343. I.D. | FG Trupp c (tmot) 343 | 5.5.44 |
| 344. I.D. | FG Trupp 344 | ? |
| 34. I.D. (mot) | FG Trupp a (mot) 345 | 27.11.42 |
| 348. I.D. | FG Trupp 348 | 15.3.44 |
| 349. I.D. | FG Trupp 349 | 5.11.43 |
| 352. I.D. | FG Trupp 352 | 4.11.43 |
| 352. I.D. | FG Trupp 352 | 14.11.43 |
| 353. I.D. | FG Trupp c (tmot) 353 | 1.12.43 |
| 355. I.D. | FG Trupp a (mot) 355 | 15.5.43 |
| 356. I.D. | FG Trupp c (tmot) 356 | 1.5.43 |
| 356. I.D. | FG Trupp a (mot) 356 | 17.5.43 |
| 357. I.D. | FG Trupp 357 | 11.11.44 |
| 359. I.D. | FG Trupp 359 | 25.11.43 |
| 361. I.D. | FG Trupp 361 | 5.11.43 |
| 362. I.D. | FG Trupp 362 | 5.11.43 |
| 362. I.D. | FG Trupp 362 | 28.3.44 |
| 363. I.D. | FG Trupp 363 | 15.12.43 |
| 363. I.D. | FG Trupp 363 | 18.12.43 |
| 365. I.D. | FG Trupp 365 | 3.6.40 |
| 367. I.D. | FG Trupp 367 | 7.10.43 |
| 367. I.D. | FG Trupp 367 | 1.12.43 |
| 369. I.D. | FG Trupp 369 (Kroat.) | ? |
| 370. I.D. | FG Trupp a (mot) 370 | 18.2.42 |
| 371. I.D. | FG Trupp a (mot) 371 | 24.3.42 |
| 373. I.D. | FG Trupp a (mot) 373 | 6.1.43 |

| | | |
|---|---|---|
| 373. I.D. (Kroat.) | FG Trupp a (mot) 373 | 13.1.43 |
| 376. I.D. | FG Trupp a (mot) 376 | 1.3.42 |
| 377. I.D. | FG Trupp a (mot) 377 | 1.3.42 |
| 383. I.D. | FG Trupp a (mot) 383 | 29.1.42 |
| 384. I.D. | FG Trupp a (mot) 384 | 25.1.42 |
| 384. I.D. | FG Trupp a (mot) 384 (neu) | 1.5.43 |
| 385. I.D. | FG Trupp a (mot) 385 | 21.1.42 |
| 386. I.D. (mot) | FG Trupp a (mot) 386 | 26.11.42 |
| 387. I.D. | FG Trupp a (mot) 387 | 27.1.42 |
| 389. I.D. | FG Trupp a (mot) 389 | 25.1.42 |
| 392. I.D. (Kroat.) | FG Trupp a (mot) 392 | 17.8.43 |
| 399. I.D. | FG Trupp 399 | 6.40 |
| 404. I.D. | FG Trupp d der O.K. I/612 | 27.11.39 |
| 404. I.D. z.b.V. | F.K. 602/FG | 20.1.40 |
| 410. I.D. | O.K. I/847 FG Gruppe | 9.8.40 |
| 410. I.D. z.b.V. | F.K. FG Gruppe | 25.11.39 |
| 413. I.D. z.b.V | F.K. 684/FG | 9.2.40 |
| 416. I.D. | FG Gruppe 990 | 4.5.43 |
| 416. I.D. | FG Gruppe 996 | 4.5.43 |
| 416. I.D. | FG Gruppe 997 | 4.5.43 |
| 416. I.D. | FG Trupp 416 | 31.5.44 |
| 421. I.D. | O.K. I/501 FG | 30.10.39 |
| 462. I.D. | FG Trupp 1462 | 15.10.44 |
| 526. I.D. | FG Trupp 316 | 26.8.39 |
| 537. I.D. | FG Trupp 10 | 28.8.39 |
| 554. I.D. | O.K. I/621 FG | 10.4.40 |
| 555. I.D. | FG Trupp 307 | 14.4.40 |
| 556. I.D. | FG Trupp a (mot) 556 | 17.3.40 |
| 556. I.D. | O.K. I/622 | 19.4.40 |
| 600. I.D. (Russ.) | FG Trupp c (tmot) 1600 | 1.12.44 |
| 606. I.D. (Stab) z.b.V. | FG Trupp c (tmot) 1606 | 8.1.45 |
| 650. I.D. (Russ.) | FG Trupp 1650 | 21.1.45 |
| 702. I.D. | FG Trupp c (tmot) 702 | 11.7.43 |
| 704. I.D. | FG Trupp 704 | 5.2.43 |
| 708. I.D. | FG Trupp 708 | 13.7.42 |
| 709. I.D. | FG Trupp 709 | 1.11.42 |
| 710. I.D. | FG Trupp 710 | 11.9.41 |
| 711. I.D. | FG Trupp c (tmot) 711 | 15.11.42 |
| 712. I.D. | FG Trupp d 712 | 24.5.42 |
| 712. I.D. | FG Trupp c (tmot) 712 | 1.11.42 |
| 715. I.D. | FG Trupp c 715 | 19.10.43 |
| 715. I.D. | FG Trupp c (mot) 715 | 11.1.44 |
| 715. I.D. | FG Trupp c (tmot) 715 | 11.5.44 |
| 716. I.D. | FG Trupp 716 | 25.7.41 |
| 719. I.D. | FG Trupp 719 | 1.12.42 |

**Jaeger Division (Light Infantry Division)**

| | | |
|---|---|---|
| 5. Jaeger Div | FG Trupp (mot) 5 | 25.8.39 |
| 5. Jaeger Div | FG Trupp (mot) 5 | 1.4.40 |
| 42. Jaeger Div | FG Trupp c (tmot) 142 | 17.1.44 |
| 99. Jaeger Div | FG Trupp (mot) 99 | 10.12.40 |
| 104. Jaeger Div | F Trupp a (mot) 104 | 10.4.43 |
| 114. Jaeger Div | FG Trupp (mot) 114 | 16.3.43 |
| 117. Jaeger Div | FG Trupp (mot) 117 | 1.4.43 |
| 118. Jaeger Div | FG Trupp (mot) 118 | 23.9.43 |

## Kavallerie Division (Cavalry Division)

| | | |
|---|---|---|
| 1. Kav.Div. | FG Trupp a (mot) 40 | 1.4.41 |

## Kossak Division (Cossack Division)

| | | |
|---|---|---|
| 1. Kos.Div. | FG Trupp 55 | 29.12.43 |

## Landwehr Division (Reserve Division)

| | | |
|---|---|---|
| 14. Ldw.Div. | FG Trupp (mot) Landwehr.14 | 26.8.39 |
| 14. Ldw.Div. | O.K. I/621 FG | 28.10.39 |

## Leichte Division (Light Infantry Division)

| | | |
|---|---|---|
| 2. le.Div. | FG Trupp 58 | 12.39 |
| 3. le.Div. | FG Trupp b (mot) 59 | 19.8.40 |
| 5. le.Div | FG Trupp a (mot) 309 | 28.1.41 |
| 5. le.Div (mot) | FG Trupp b (mot) 309 | 28.1.41 |
| 90. le.Div. | FG Trupp 90 le.Div. (behelfsmaessiger) | ? |
| 90. le.Div. | FG Trupp 97 | 17.2.41 |
| 101. le.Div. | FG Trupp (mot) 101 | 10.12.40 |
| 999. le.Div. | FG Trupp b (mot) 999 | 14.11.42 |

## Luftwaffe Felddivision (Air Force Field Division)

| | | |
|---|---|---|
| 1. Luftwaffe Felddiv. | FG Trupp d 1101 | 3.8.43 |
| 2. Luftwaffe Felddiv. | FG Trupp d 1102 | 3.8.43 |
| 2. Luftwaffe Felddiv. | FG Trupp c (tmot) 62 | 6.10.43 |
| 3. Luftwaffe Felddiv. | FG Trupp d 1103 | 3.8.43 |
| 4. Luftwaffe Felddiv. | FG Trupp d 1104 | 3.8.43 |
| 5. Luftwaffe Felddiv. | FG Trupp d 1105 | 3.8.43 |
| 6. Luftwaffe Felddiv. | FG Trupp d 1106 | 3.8.43 |
| 9. Luftwaffe Felddiv. | FG Trupp d 1109 | 3.8.43 |
| 10. Luftwaffe Felddiv. | FG Trupp d 1110 | 3.8.43 |
| 11. Luftwaffe Felddiv. | FG Trupp d 1111 | 3.8.43 |
| 12. Luftwaffe Felddiv. | FG Trupp der 21. Luftwaffe Felddiv. | 19.11.42 |
| 12. Luftwaffe Felddiv. | FG Trupp d 1112 | 3.8.43 |
| 13. Luftwaffe Felddiv. | FG Trupp d 1113 | 3.8.43 |
| 14. Luftwaffe Felddiv. | FG Trupp d 1114 | 3.8.43 |
| 15. Luftwaffe Felddiv. | FG Trupp d 1115 | 3.8.43 |
| 16. Luftwaffe Felddiv. | FG Trupp d der 16. Luftwaffe Felddiv. | 1.12.42 |
| 17. Luftwaffe Felddiv. | FG Trupp d 1117 | 3.8.43 |
| 18. Luftwaffe Felddiv. | FG Trupp d 1118 | 3.8.43 |
| 19. Luftwaffe Felddiv. | FG Trupp d 1119 | 3.8.43 |
| 19. Luftwaffe Felddiv. | FG Trupp der 19. Luftwaffe Felddiv. | 21.8.43 |
| 20. Luftwaffe Felddiv. | FG Trupp d 1120 | 3.8.43 |
| 21. Luftwaffe Felddiv. | FG Trupp der 21. Luftwaffe Felddiv. | 2.1.43 |
| 21. Luftwaffe Felddiv. | FG Trupp d 1121 | 3.8.43 |
| 22. Luftwaffe Felddiv. | FG Trupp d 1122 | 3.8.43 |

## Panzer Division (Armored Division)

| | | |
|---|---|---|
| 1. Pz.Div. | FG Trupp 58 | 9.9.38 |
| 1. Pz.Div. | FG Trupp b (mot) 81 | 19.8.39 |
| 2. Pz.Div. | FG Trupp 82 | 16.8.39 |
| 3. Pz.Div. | FG Trupp b (mot) 83 | 18.8.39 |
| 4. Pz.Div. | FG Trupp b (mot) 84 | 1.8.39 |
| 5. Pz.Div. | FG Trupp b 85 | 22.8.39 |
| 6. Pz.Div. | FG Trupp b (mot) 57 | 19.8.39 |
| 7. Pz.Div. | FG Trupp 58 | 10.11.39 |
| 8. Pz.Div. | FG Trupp b (mot) 59 | 18.10.39 |
| 9. Pz.Div. | FG Trupp 60 | 20.8.39 |
| 9. Pz.Div. | FG Trupp b (mot) 60 | 28.3.44 |

| | | |
|---|---|---|
| 10. Pz.Div | FG Trupp b (mot) 10 | 28.3.44 |
| 10. Pz.Div. (Stab) | FG Trupp b (mot) 90 | 1.11.39 |
| 11. Pz.Div. | FG Trupp b (mot) 61 | 29.7.40 |
| 11. Pz.Div. | FG Trupp b (mot) 61 | 13.8.40 |
| 12. Pz.Div. | FG Trupp b (mot) 2 | 10.1.41 |
| 13. Pz.Div. | FG Trupp b (mot) 13 | ? 44 |
| 14. Pz.Div. | FG Trupp b (mot) 4 | 8.8.40 |
| 15. Pz.Div. | FG Trupp (mot) 33 | 1.11.40 |
| 16. Pz.Div. | FG Trupp b (mot) 16 | 1.8.40 |
| 17. Pz.Div. | FG Trupp b (mot) 27 | 11.10.400 |
| 18. Pz.Div. | FG Trupp b (mot) 88 | 1.12.40 |
| 19. Pz.Div. | FG Trupp b (mot) 19 | 1.11.40 |
| 21. Pz.Div. | FG Trupp 200 | 15.8.41 |
| 21. Pz.Div. | FG Trupp (mot) 200 | 4.10.41 |
| 21. Pz.Div. | FG Trupp (mot) 200 | 15.7.43 |
| 21. Pz.Div. | FG Trupp (mot) 200 (neu) | 1.1.44 |
| 23. Pz.Div. | FG Trupp 128 | 13.5.43 |
| 24. Pz.Div. | FG Trupp b (mot) 40 | 4.1.42 |
| 25. Pz.Div. | FG Trupp c (tmot) 87 | 15.1.43 |
| 26. Pz.Div. | FG Trupp 93 | 14.10.42 |
| 26. Pz.Div. | FG Trupp b (mot) 93 | 19.10.42 |
| 27. Pz.Div. | FG Trupp 127 | 23.10.42 |
| 27. Pz.Div. | FG Trupp a (mot) 127 | 2.11.42 |
| 116. Pz.Div. | FG Trupp b (mot) 66 | 28.3.44 |
| Div. Hermann Goering | FG Trupp b (mot) 1000 Hermann Goering | 3.8.43 |
| Fuehrer Begleit Div. | FG Trupp 120 | 24.1.45 |
| Grossdeutschland Div. | FG Kp Grossdeutschland | 20.3.42 |
| Pz.Div. Feldherrnhalle | FG Trupp b Feldherrnhalle | 7.11.44 |
| Pz.Div. Holstein | FG Trupp 144 | 2.2.45 |
| Pz.Div. Jueterbog | FG Trupp "Jueterbog" | 20.2.45 |
| Pz.Div. Kempf | FG Trupp b (mot) 90 | 25.7.39 |
| Pz.Div. Schlesien | FG Trupp Schlesien | ?.45 |
| Pz.Gruppe 2 | FG Trupp b (mot) 419 | 16.11.40 |
| Pz.Gruppe 3 | FG Trupp b 415 | 16.11.40 |
| Pz.Gruppe 3 | Stab, 1.u.2.Kp., FG Abt 551 | 24.8.41 |
| Pz.Lehr Div. | FG Trupp/Pz Lehr Div | 11.12.43 |
| Pz.Lehr Div. | FG Trupp b (mot)/Pz Lehr Div | 17.2.44 |

**Panzerersatz Abteilung (Armor Personnel Replacement Battalion)**

| | | |
|---|---|---|
| Pz.Ers.Abt. (Hamm) | FG Trupp (mot) 309 | 26.8.39 |

**Panzergrenadier Division (Armored Infantry Division)**

| | | |
|---|---|---|
| 15. Pz.Gr.Div. | FG Trupp 33 | 22.7.43 |
| 18. Pz.Gr.Div. | FG Trupp 18 | 12.11.44 |
| 25. Pz.Gr.Div. | FG Trupp 25 | 29.10.44 |
| 90. Pz.Gr.Div. | FG Trupp 190 | 6.7.43 |
| Pz.Gr.Div.Brandenburg | FG Trupp "Brandenburg" | 13.9.44 |
| Pz.Gr.Div.Feldherrnhalle | FG Trupp b Feldherrnhalle | 14.6.43 |
| Pz.Gr.Div.Feldherrnhalle | FG Trupp b (mot) "Feldherrnhalle" | 17.7.43 |
| Pz.Gr.Div.Grossdeutschland | FG KP Grossdeutschland | 13.12.44 |

**Reservedivision (Reserve Division)**

| | | |
|---|---|---|
| 148. Res.Div. | FG Trupp d (tmot) 1048 | 15.5.44 |
| 156. Res.Div. | FG Trupp c (tmot) 1056 | 26.11.42 |
| 156. Res.Div. | FG Trupp d 1056 | 25.2.43 |

| | | |
|---|---|---|
| 158. Res.Div. | FG Trupp (tmot) der 158. Res.Div. | 7.2.43 |
| 160. Res.Div. | FG Trupp 905 | 8.5.42 |
| 171. Res.Div. | FG Trupp 1071 | 7.3.43 |
| 189. Res.Div. | FG Trupp c (tmot) 189 | 23.2.43 |
| 189. Res.Div. | FG Trupp c (tmot) 356 | 23.2.43 |
| 191. Res.Div. | FG Trupp d 1091 | 10.3.43 |

**Sicherheitsdivision (Security Division)**

| | | |
|---|---|---|
| 281. Sich.Div. | FG Trupp c (tmot) 600 | 18.10.44 |
| 281. Sich.Div. | FG Trupp c (tmot) 281 | 11.11.44 |
| 444. Sich.Div. | FG Trupp 360 | 21.5.44 |
| 444. Sich.Div. | FG Trupp 442 z.b.V. | 24.5.44 |

**Ski.Jaegerdivision (Light Ski Division)**

| | | |
|---|---|---|
| 1. Ski.Jg.Div. | FG Trupp 152 | 16.11.44 |

**SS-Polizeidivision (SS Police Division)**

| | | |
|---|---|---|
| SS-Pol.Div. | FG Trupp 426 | 10.11.39 |
| SS-Pol.Div. | FG Trupp 300 | 18.11.39 |
| SS-Pol.Div. | O.K. I/621 FG | 5.2.40 |

**Sturmdivision (Storm Division)**

| | | |
|---|---|---|
| 78. Sturm Div. | FG Trupp (mot) 178 | 15.7.43 |
| Sturmdiv. Rhodos | FG Trupp a (mot) 999 | 16.7.43 |
| Sturmdiv. Rhodos | FG Trupp c (tmot) 999 | 15.2.44 |

**Ungarn Division (Hungarian Division)**

| | | |
|---|---|---|
| 1. Ung.Div.Kossuth | FG Trupp 101 (neu) | 6.1.45 |

**Volksgrenadier Division (Infantry Division)**

| | | |
|---|---|---|
| 6. Vo.Gr.Div. | FG Trupp 6 | 18.7.44 |
| 9. Vo.Gr.Div. | FG Trupp 9 | 27.10.44 |
| 18. Vo.Gr.Div. | FG Trupp c (tmot) 1818 | 8.9.44 |
| 18. Vo.Gr.Div. | FG Trupp 1818 | 13.9.44 |
| 26. Vo.Gr.Div. | FG Trupp 26 | 17.9.44 |
| 31. Vo.Gr.Div. | FG Trupp 31 | 18.7.44 |
| 45. Vo.Gr.Div. | FG Trupp c (tmot) 45 | 18.7.44 |
| 47. Vo.Gr.Div. | FG Trupp 147 | 17.9.44 |
| 62. Vo.Gr.Div. | FG Trupp 162 | 22.9.44 |
| 78. Vo.Gr.Div. | FG Trupp 178 | 18.7.44 |
| 79. Vo.Gr.Div. | FG Trupp 179 | 27.10.44 |
| 167. Vo.Gr.Div. | FG Trupp 167 | 2.9.44 |
| 183. Vo.Gr.Div. | FG Trupp 219 | 17.9.44 |
| 212. Vo.Gr.Div. | FG Trupp 212 | 17.9.44 |
| 246. Vo.Gr.Div. | FG Trupp 246 | 17.9.44 |
| 256. Vo.Gr.Div. | FG Trupp 256 | 17.9.44 |
| 257. Vo.Gr.Div. | FG Trupp c 257 | 13.10.44 |
| 276. Vo.Gr.Div. | FG Trupp 276 | 4.9.44 |
| 276. Vo.Gr.Div. | FG Trupp c (tmot) 1276 | 8.10.44 |
| 320. Vo.Gr.Div. | FG Trupp 320 | 27.10.44 |
| 326. Vo.Gr.Div. | FG Trupp 326 | 4.9.44 |
| 337. Vo.Gr.Div. | FG Trupp 337 | 17.9.44 |
| 340. Vo.Gr.Div. | FG Trupp 340 | 4.9.44 |
| 349. Vo.Gr.Div. | FG Trupp 349 | 14.9.44 |
| 352. Vo.Gr.Div. | FG Trupp der 352 Vo.Gr.Div. | 21.9.44 |
| 361. Vo.Gr.Div. | FG Trupp 361 | 28.3.44 |
| 361. Vo.Gr.Div. | FG Trupp c (tmot) 361 | 26.9.44 |
| 363. Vo.Gr.Div. | FG Trupp 363 | 17.9.44 |
| 560. Vo.Gr.Div. | FG Trupp 1560 | 10.8.44 |
| 562. Vo.Gr.Div. | FG Trupp 1562 | 15.10.44 |

| | | |
|---|---|---|
| 564. Vo.Gr.Div. | FG Trupp 1564 | 25.8.44 |
| 565. Vo.Gr.Div. | FG Trupp 1565 | 25.8.44 |
| 566. Vo.Gr.Div. | FG Trupp 1566 | 25.8.44 |
| 567. Vo.Gr.Div. | FG Trupp 1567 | 25.8.44 |
| 568. Vo.Gr.Div. | FG Trupp 1568 | 25.8.44 |
| 569. Vo.Gr.Div. | FG Trupp 1569 | 25.8.44 |
| 570. Vo.Gr.Div. | FG Trupp 1570 | 25.8.44 |
| 571. Vo.Gr.Div. | FG Trupp 1571 | 25.8.44 |
| 572. Vo.Gr.Div. | FG Trupp 1572 | 25.8.44 |
| 573. Vo.Gr.Div. | FG Trupp 1573 | 25.8.44 |
| 574. Vo.Gr.Div. | FG Trupp 1574 | 25.8.44 |
| 574. Vo.Gr.Div. | FG Trupp 277 | 4.9.44 |
| 575. Vo.Gr.Div. | FG Trupp 1575 | 25.8.44 |
| 575. Vo.Gr.Div. | FG Trupp 272 | 17.9.44 |
| 576. Vo.Gr.Div. | FG Trupp 1576 | 25.8.44 |
| 576. Vo.Gr.Div. | FG Trupp 271 | 17.9.44 |
| 577. Vo.Gr.Div. | FG Trupp 1577 | 25.8.44 |
| 578. Vo.Gr.Div. | FG Trupp 1578 | 25.8.44 |
| 579. Vo.Gr.Div. | FG Trupp 1579 | 25.8.44 |
| 580. Vo.Gr.Div. | FG Trupp 1580 | 25.8.44 |
| 581. Vo.Gr.Div. | FG Trupp 1581 | 25.8.44 |
| 582. Vo.Gr.Div. | FG Trupp 1582 | 25.8.44 |
| 708. Vo.Gr.Div. | FG Trupp 708 | 4.9.44 |
| Vo.Gr.Div. Grossgoerschen | FG Trupp c 257 | 9.10.44 |

## FELDGENDARMERIE

**Feldgendarmerie Abteilung (Military Police Battalion)**

| | | |
|---|---|---|
| Feldgendarmerie Abteilung 541 | FG Trupp b (mot) 419 | 17.2.43 |

**Feldgendarmerie Ersatz Regiment (Military Police Replacement Regiment)**

| | | |
|---|---|---|
| Feldgendarmerie Ersatz Regiment 1 | FG Staffeln 1001 | 3.6.43 |
| Feldgendarmerie Ersatz Regiment 1 | FG Staffeln 1002 | 3.6.43 |
| Feldgendarmerie Ersatz Regiment 1 | FG Staffeln 1003 | 3.6.43 |
| Feldgendarmerie Ersatz Regiment 1 | FG Staffeln 1004 | 3.6.43 |
| Feldgendarmerie Ersatz Regiment 1 | FG Staffeln 1005 | 3.6.43 |
| Feldgendarmerie Ersatz Regiment 1 | FG Staffeln 1006 | 3.6.43 |
| Feldgendarmerie Ersatz Regiment 1 | FG Staffeln 1007 | 3.6.43 |

**Feldgendarmerie Asbildungs Abteilung (Military Police Training Battalion)**

| | | |
|---|---|---|
| Feldgendarmerie Ausb.Abt.II | FG Trupp d 924 | 1.2.43 |

## KOMMANDO

**Befehlshaber/Militaerbefehlshaber (Commander/Military Commander)**

| | | |
|---|---|---|
| Befh.Suedgriechenland | Stab, FG Abt (mot) 501 | 1.8.41 |
| Befh.Suedgriechenland | 3.Kp. FG Abt (mot) 501 | 1.8.41 |
| Befh.Heeresgebiet Mitte | FG Abt (mot) 690 | 3.1.41 |
| Befh.Nordost Frankreich | FG Trupp a (mot) 925 | 27.4.43 |
| Befh.Nordost Frankreich | FG Trupp b (mot) 688 | 10.7.44 |
| Befh.Nordw.Frankreich | FG Trupp d 691 | 1.11.43 |
| Befh.Nordw.Frankreich | FG Trupp b (mot) 685 | 10.7.44 |
| Befh.Sudw.Frankreich | FG Trupp d 744 | 30.4.43 |
| Befh.Sudw.Frankreich | FG Trupp a 752 | 1.5.43 |
| Befh.Sudw.Frankreich | FG Trupp d 692 | 16.9.43 |
| Befh.Sudw.Frankreich | FG Trupp b (mot) 687 | 10.7.44 |
| Befh.der dtsch.Tr.i.Daenemark | FG Trupp c (tmot) 603 | 25.9.41 |

| | | |
|---|---|---|
| Befh.der dtsch.Tr.i.Kroatien | 2.Kp. FG Abt (mot) 501 | 27.7.42 |
| Befh.der dtsch.Tr.i.Transnistrien | Stab, FG Abt (mot) 698 | 1.3.44 |
| Befh.der dtsch.Tr.i.Transnistrien | 1.Kp. FG Abt (mot) 698 | 1.3.44 |
| Befh.der rueckw.H.Geb.101 | Stab, FG Abt (mot) 691 | 15.3.41 |
| Befh.der rueckw.H.Geb.101 | 1.Kp. FG Abt (mot) 691 | 15.3.41 |
| Befh.der rueckw.H.Geb.101 | 2.Kp. FG Abt (mot) 691 | 15.3.41 |
| Befh.der rueckw.H.Geb.101 | 3.Kp. FG Abt (mot) 691 | 15.3.41 |
| Befh.der rueckw.H.Geb.B. | FG Abt (mot) 692 | 11.2.41 |
| Befh. Nordwest Fr. | FG Trupp c (tmot) 579 | 1.4.43 |
| Befh. Nordwest Fr. | FG Trupp a (mot) 754 | 22.4.43 |
| Befh. Oslo Suedwest | FG Trupp (mot) 571 | 26.8.40 |
| Dtsch.Befh.H.Geb.Ungarn | FG Trupp d 508 | 24.10.44 |
| Dtsch.Befh.i.Westungarn | FG Trupp d 508 | 9.10.44 |
| Kommand.Gen.u.Befh.Sudgriechenland | 3.Kp. FG Abt (mot) 501 | 21.6.43 |
| Mil.Befh.Serbien | F.K. V/809 FG Gruppe | 22.4.41 |
| Mil.Befh.Serbien | O.K. I/832 FG Gruppe | 22.4.41 |
| Mil.Befh.Serbien | O.K. I/857 FG Gruppe | 26.4.41 |
| Mil.Befh.Serbien | O.K. I (V)/833 FG Gruppe | 28.4.41 |
| Mil.Befh.Serbien | K.K. I/857 (V) FG Gruppe | 1.5.41 |
| Mil.Befh.Serbien | O.K. I/838 FG Gruppe | 2.5.41 |
| Mil.Befh.Serbien | 1.Kp. FG Abt (mot) 501 | 17.6.41 |
| Mil.Befh.Serbien | O.K. I/861 FG Gruppe | 3.7.41 |
| Mil.Befh.Serbien | O.K. I (V)/838 FG Gruppe | 3.7.41 |
| Mil.Befh.Serbien | O.K. I (V) B/838 FG Gruppe | 18.7.41 |
| Mil.Befh.Serbien | K.K. I/833 FG Trupp d | 17.8.41 |
| Mil.Befh.Serbien | K.K. I (V)/867 FG Trupp | 17.8.41 |
| Mil.Befh.Serbien | FG Trupp c (tmot) der O.K. I(V) B/838 | 17.8.41 |
| Mil.Befh.Serbien | FG Trupp c (tmot) 857 | 15.11.41 |
| Mil.Befh.Serbien | FG Trupp c (tmot) 859 | 15.11.41 |
| Mil.Befh.Serbien | FG Trupp c (tmot) 861 | 15.11.41 |
| Mil.Befh.Serbien | FG Trupp d 865 | 15.11.41 |
| Mil.Befh.Serbien | FG Trupp d 867 | 15.11.41 |
| Mil.Befh.Serbien | FG Trupp c (tmot) 868 | 15.11.41 |
| Mil.Befh.i.Fr. | O.K. I/637 FG | 15.10.39 |
| Mil.Befh.i.Fr. | O.K.II/747 FG Gruppe | 31.5.40 |
| Mil.Befh.i.Fr. | FG Trupp d der K.K. 773 | 3.6.40 |
| Mil.Befh.i.Fr. | O.K. 626/FG Gruppe | 16.6.40 |
| Mil.Befh.i.Fr. | O.K. I/695 (V) FG | 12.7.40 |
| Mil.Befh.i.Fr. | O.K.II/667/FG | 25.7.40 |
| Mil.Befh.i.Fr. | O.K. I(V) 791 FG Gruppe | 1.8.40 |
| Mil.Befh.i.Fr. | O.K. I/667/FG | 6.9.40 |
| Mil.Befh.i.Fr. | K.K. I/623 | 10.9.40 |
| Mil.Befh.i.Fr. | K.K. 637 (V) FG | 10.9.40 |
| Mil.Befh.i.Fr. | K.K. I/649 FG Trupp d (mot) | 14.9.40 |
| Mil.Befh.i.Fr. | FG Trupp 667 der K.K. 667 | 28.9.40 |
| Mil.Befh.i.Fr. | K.K.II/744 FG Gruppe | 25.10.40 |
| Mil.Befh.i.Fr. | FG Trupp d.K.K. 626 | 31.10.40 |
| Mil.Befh.i.Fr. | K.K 623/FG | 4.11.40 |
| Mil.Befh.i.Fr. | FG Trupp d der K.K.747 | 27.12.40 |
| Mil.Befh.i.Fr. | FG Trupp d der K.K. 791 | 27.12.40 |
| Mil.Befh.i.Fr. | FG Trupp c (mot) 623 | 1.4.41 |
| Mil.Befh.i.Fr. | O.K. I/542 FG | 17.8.41 |
| Mil.Befh.i.Fr. | FG Trupp 543 | 9.9.41 |

| | | |
|---|---|---|
| Mil.Befh.i.Fr. | FG Trupp d (mot) der K.K. 695 | 9.9.41 |
| Mil.Befh.i.Fr. | FG Trupp c (tmot) 623 | 15.9.41 |
| Mil.Befh.i.Fr. | FG Trupp a (mot) 903 | 29.9.41 |
| Mil.Befh.i.Fr. | FG Trupp c (tmot) 923 | 29.9.41 |
| Mil.Befh.i.Fr. | FG Trupp c (tmot) 933 | 29.9.41 |
| Mil.Befh.i.Fr. | FG Trupp a (mot) 913 | 1.10.41 |
| Mil.Befh.i.Fr. | FG Trupp II d (mot) der F.K. 669 | 6.10.41 |
| Mil.Befh.i.Fr. | FG Trupp 649 bei der K.K. 649 | 15.11.41 |
| Mil.Befh.i.Fr. | FG Trupp 667 | 15.11.41 |
| Mil.Befh.i.Fr. | FG Trupp 542 | 27.11.41 |
| Mil.Befh.i.Fr. | FG Trupp 747 der K.K. 747 | 27.11.41 |
| Mil.Befh.i.Fr. | FG Trupp 791 der K.K. 791 | 27.11.41 |
| Mil.Befh.i.Fr. | FG Trupp 896 | 27.11.41 |
| Mil.Befh.i.Fr. | FG Trupp d (mot) 699 | 1.12.41 |
| Mil.Befh.i.Fr. | FG Trupp 747 | 5.1.42 |
| Mil.Befh.i.Fr. | FG Trupp 649 | 15.1.42 |
| Mil.Befh.i.Fr. | FG Trupp 791 der F.K. 684 | 20.6.42 |
| Mil.Befh.i.Fr. | FG Trupp d 693 | 16.9.43 |
| Mil.Befh.i.Fr.,Bez.Chef A | F.K. 608(V) FG Gruppe | 3.7.40 |
| Mil.Befh.i.Fr.,Bez.Chef A | F.K. 684/FG | 4.7.40 |
| Mil.Befh.i.Fr.,Bez.Chef A | FG Trupp a (mot) F.K.684 | 27.12.40 |
| Mil.Befh.i.Fr.,Bez.Chef A | FG Trupp 684 | 1.12.41 |
| Mil.Befh.i.Fr.,Bez.Chef C | F.K. 608(V) FG Gruppe | 13.9.40 |
| Mil.Befh.i.Fr.,Bez.Chef C | K.K. 888/FG | 8.10.40 |
| Mil.Befh.i.Fr.,Bez.Chef C | O.K. I (V)/833 FG Gruppe | 24.11.40 |
| Mil.Befh.i.Fr.,Bez.Chef C | FG Trupp 608 | 15.11.41 |
| Mil.Befh.i.Fr.,Bez.Chef C | FG Trupp 888 | 15.11.41 |
| Mil.Befh.i.Fr.,Mil.Verw.Bez.A | F.K. 756 FG Gruppe | 3.6.40 |
| Mil.Befh.i.Fr.,Mil.Verw.Bez.A | F.K. 723/FG | 29.7.40 |
| Mil.Befh.i.Fr.,Mil.Verw.Bez.A | FG Trupp der F.K. 758 | 30.10.40 |
| Mil.Befh.i.Fr.,Mil.Verw.Bez.A | FG Trupp a (mot) der F.K. 723 | 15.11.40 |
| Mil.Befh.i.Fr.,Mil.Verw.Bez.A | O.K. I/847 FG Trupp | 31.1.41 |
| Mil.Befh.i.Fr.,Mil.Verw.Bez.A | FG Trupp 723 | 15.11.41 |
| Mil.Befh.i.Fr.,Mil.Verw.Bez.A | FG Trupp 876 | 26.11.41 |
| Mil.Befh.i.Fr.,Mil.Verw.Bez.A | FG Trupp a (mot) 902 | 9.1.42 |
| Mil.Befh.i.Fr.,Mil.Verw.Bez.B | O.K. I/823 FG Gruppe | 7.8.40 |
| Mil.Befh.i.Fr.,Mil.Verw.Bez.B | F.K. 756 FG Gruppe | 18.9.40 |
| Mil.Befh.i.Fr.,Mil.Verw.Bez.B | F.K. 756 FG Trupp | 21.9.40 |
| Mil.Befh.i.Fr.,Mil.Verw.Bez.B | FG Trupp a (mot) 756 | 22.9.41 |
| Mil.Befh.i.Fr.,Mil.Verw.Bez.C | O.K. I/562 FG | 1.7.40 |
| Mil.Befh.i.Fr.,Mil.Verw.Bez.C | FG der F.K.509 | 1.9.40 |
| Mil.Befh.i.Fr.,Mil.Verw.Bez.C | K.K. I/562 FG | 10.9.40 |
| Mil.Befh.i.Fr.,Mil.Verw.Bez.C | K.K. I/563 FG | 10.9.40 |
| Mil.Befh.i.Fr.,Mil.Verw.Bez.C | K.K. 745 FG | 10.9.40 |
| Mil.Befh.i.Fr.,Mil.Verw.Bez.C | O.K. I(V) 891 FG | 21.9.40 |
| Mil.Befh.i.Fr.,Mil.Verw.Bez.C | K.K. 891 FG | 9.11.40 |
| Mil.Befh.i.Fr.,Mil.Verw.Bez.C | FG Trupp c (tmot) der F.K. 509 | 17.8.41 |
| Mil.Befh.i.Fr.,Mil.Verw.Bez.C | FG Trupp 509 | 15.11.41 |
| Mil.Befh.i.Fr.,Mil.Verw.Bez.C | FG Trupp 562 | 15.11.41 |
| Mil.Befh.i.Fr.,Mil.Verw.Bez.C | FG Trupp 563 | 15.11.41 |
| Mil.Befh.i.Fr.,Mil.Verw.Bez.C | FG Trupp 745 | 15.11.41 |
| Mil.Befh.i.Fr.,Mil.Verw.Bez.C | FG Trupp 889 | 15.11.41 |
| Mil.Befh.i.Fr.,Mil.Verw.Bez.C | FG Trupp 891 | 15.11.41 |
| Mil.Befh.i.Fr.,Mil.Verw.Bez.C | FG Trupp d 891 | 15.1.42 |

| | | |
|---|---|---|
| Mil.Befh.i.Fr.,Mil.Verw.Bez.C | FG Trupp 721 | 24.7.42 |
| Mil.Befh.i.Fr.,Mil.Verw.Bez.C | FG Gruppe 998 | 14.12.42 |
| Mil.Befh.i.Krakau | FG Abt (mot) 685 (mit 1,2,3 Kp) | 8.10.39 |
| Mil.Befh.i.Nordostfr.,Bez.Chef C | FG Gruppe bei der F.K.599 | 2.3.41 |
| Mil.Befh.i.Serbien | O.K. I/823 FG Gruppe | 14.4.41 |
| Mil.Befh.i.Serbien | FG Gruppe bei der F.K.599 | 17.4.41 |
| Mil.Befh.i.Serbien | F.K. (V)816 FG Gruppe | 23.4.41 |
| Mil.Befh.i.Serbien | F.K. 610/V/FG Gruppe | 24.4.41 |
| Mil.Befh.i.Serbien | FG Trupp d der K.K. 847 | 17.8.41 |
| Mil.Befh.i.Serbien | FG Trupp d 610 | 8.10.41 |
| Mil.Befh.i.Serbien | FG Trupp d 870 | 15.11.41 |
| Mil.Befh.i.Serbien | FG Trupp d 871 | 15.11.41 |
| Mil.Befh.i.Serbien | FG Trupp d 875 | 15.11.41 |
| Mil.Befh.i.Serbien | FG Trupp d 869 | 1.12.41 |
| Mil.Befh.i.Serbien | FG Trupp c (tmot) 871 | 26.5.42 |
| Mil.Befhl.Westpr.-Danzig | FG Trupp 584 | 15.9.39 |

**Deutsche Standortoffizier Neapel (German Garrison Commander Naples)**

| | | |
|---|---|---|
| Deutsche Standortoffz.Neapel | FG Gruppe Neapel | 19.11.42 |

**Deutsche Wehrmacht in Italien (German Armed Forces in Italy)**

| | | |
|---|---|---|
| Deutsch.Wehrm.i.Italien | FG Trupp d 559 | 6.3.44 |
| Deutsch.Wehrm.i.Italien | FG Trupp d 565 | 6.3.44 |
| Deutsch.Wehrm.i.Italien | FG Trupp d (mot) 1142 | 15.5.44 |
| Kdtr.d.Befhl.Saarpfalz | FG Trupp 584 | 1.7.40 |

**Feldkommandantur (Military Administration Headquarters)**

| | | |
|---|---|---|
| Feldkommandantur 31 | Stab, 1.-3.Kp., FG Abt 551 | 15.10.42 |
| Feldkommandantur 197 | FG Trupp d 960 | 17.2.44 |
| Feldkommandantur 243 | FG Trupp d (tmot) 1145 | 9.8.44 |
| Feldkommandantur 245 | FG Trupp d 245 | 3.10.42 |
| Feldkommandantur 245 | FG Trupp d (tmot) 1146 | 9.8.44 |
| Feldkommandantur 509 | O.K. I/641 FG | 9.7.40 |
| Feldkommandantur 515 | F.K.515/FG | 10.9.39 |
| Feldkommandantur 517 | FG Trupp a (mot) 517 | 25.11.40 |
| Feldkommandantur 517 | FG Trupp c (tmot) 753 | 30.12.41 |
| Feldkommandantur 520 | FG Trupp c (tmot) 821 | ? |
| Feldkommandantur 520 | FG Trupp a (mot) 6 | 13.9.41 |
| Feldkommandantur 528 (Tours) | FG Trupp a (mot) 246 | 27.11.40 |
| Feldkommandantur 529 | FG Trupp 210 | 11.6.41 |
| Feldkommandantur 529 | FG Trupp 211 | 31.10.41 |
| Feldkommandantur 531 | FG Trupp a (mot) 225 | 4.11.40 |
| Feldkommandantur 531 | FG Trupp 608 | 15.1.42 |
| Feldkommandantur 538 | FG Trupp a 183 | 15.11.40 |
| Feldkommandantur 538 | O.K.II/703 FG Trupp | 1.12.40 |
| Feldkommandantur 538 | FG Trupp a (mot) 183 | 1.12.40 |
| Feldkommandantur 549 | O.K. I/544 FG | 7.4.40 |
| Feldkommandantur 560 | O.K.(V)I/621 | 21.7.40 |
| Feldkommandantur 560 | K.K. 621/FG | 10.9.40 |
| Feldkommandantur 560 | FG Trupp 621 | 15.11.41 |
| Feldkommandantur 564 (Toulose) | FG Trupp a (mot) 929 | 23.3.43 |
| Feldkommandantur 578 | O.K.II/703 FG Trupp | 11.5.40 |
| Feldkommandantur 581 | FG Trupp 511 | 15.7.40 |
| Feldkommandantur 581 | FG Trupp 806 | 10.9.40 |
| Feldkommandantur 588 | FG Trupp (mot) 216 | 31.10.40 |
| Feldkommandantur 588 | FG Trupp 588 | 6.6.41 |
| Feldkommandantur 588 (Tours) | FG Trupp a (mot) 246 | 2.5.41 |

| | | |
|---|---|---|
| Feldkommandantur 588 (Tours) | FG Trupp a (mot) 588 | 6.6.41 |
| Feldkommandantur 589 | O.K. I/641 FG | 21.7.40 |
| Feldkommandantur 589 | K.K. 641/FG | 10.9.40 |
| Feldkommandantur 589 | FG Trupp 589/II der F.K. 589 | 17.9.41 |
| Feldkommandantur 589 | FG Trupp 585 der F.K. 589 | 27.11.41 |
| Feldkommandantur 589 | FG Trupp 641 | 5.1.42 |
| Feldkommandantur 590 | FG Trupp | 42 |
| Feldkommandantur 591 | FG Trupp der F.K. 591 | 1.12.40 |
| Feldkommandantur 591 | FG Trupp 901 | 9.1.42 |
| Feldkommandantur 599 | FG Trupp (mot) 215 | 5.11.40 |
| Feldkommandantur 602 | O.K. I/645 FG | 24.5.40 |
| Feldkommandantur 602 | FG Trupp a (mot) der F.K. 602 | 14.11.40 |
| Feldkommandantur 602 | FG Trupp 604 | 27.11.41 |
| Feldkommandantur 605 | FG Trupp d 1122 | 12.5.44 |
| Feldkommandantur 606 | O.K.II/703 FG Trupp | 19.4.40 |
| Feldkommandantur 608 | O.K. I/645 FG | 8.3.40 |
| Feldkommandantur 610 | F.K. 610/V/FG Gruppe | 27.11.39 |
| Feldkommandantur 615 | FG Trupp der F.K. 615 | 10.3.40 |
| Feldkommandantur 665 | FG Trupp a (mot) 616 | 22.6.42 |
| Feldkommandantur 669 | FG Trupp a (mot) 208 | 1.11.40 |
| Feldkommandantur 673 | FG Trupp der F.K. 673 | 29.1.40 |
| Feldkommandantur 674 | FG Trupp c (tmot) 873 | 4.5.44 |
| Feldkommandantur 677 (Poitiers) | FG Trupp a (mot) 616 | 19.1.42 |
| Feldkommandantur 678 | FG Trupp der F.K. 678 | 25.11.40 |
| Feldkommandantur 678 | FG Trupp d 801 der F.K. 678 | 15.1.42 |
| Feldkommandantur 680 | FG Trupp 205 | ? |
| Feldkommandantur 680 | O.K.II/781 FG | 9.7.40 |
| Feldkommandantur 680 | F.K. 680 FG Gruppe | 8.8.40 |
| Feldkommandantur 680 | K.K. 781 FG Trupp | 11.10.40 |
| Feldkommandantur 680 | FG Trupp 680 | 5.8.41 |
| Feldkommandantur 681 | FG Trupp a (mot) 820 | ? |
| Feldkommandantur 682 | FG Trupp a (mot) 7 | ? |
| Feldkommandantur 684 | FG Trupp d der O.K. I(V)/612 | 16.6.40 |
| Feldkommandantur 684 | FG Trupp d der K.K. 612 | 15.9.40 |
| Feldkommandantur 684 | FG Trupp 612 der K.K. 612 | 15.11.41 |
| Feldkommandantur 684 | FG Trupp 612 der F.K. 684 | 20.6.42 |
| Feldkommandantur 722 | F.K. 722/Gendarmerie | 20.5.40 |
| Feldkommandantur 722 (St.Lo) | K.K. 583/FG | 10.9.40 |
| Feldkommandantur 724 | FG Trupp b F.K. 724 | ? |
| Feldkommandantur 724 | FG Trupp c (tmot) 874 | 4.5.44 |
| Feldkommandantur 725 | FG Trupp d 1123 | 12.5.44 |
| Feldkommandantur 748 | FG Trupp 511 | 29.4.41 |
| Feldkommandantur 748 | FG Trupp 872 | 23.12.41 |
| Feldkommandantur 750 (Vannes) | O.K.II/592 FG | 27.7.40 |
| Feldkommandantur 750 (Vannes) | FG Trupp 592 | 31.10.40 |
| Feldkommandantur 751 | FG Trupp der F.K. 751 | 1.12.40 |
| Feldkommandantur 751 | FG Trupp a (mot) 751 | 4.11.41 |
| Feldkommandantur 752 | FG Trupp der F.K. 752 | 16.6.40 |
| Feldkommandantur 752 | FG Trupp a (mot) 251 | 5.9.40 |
| Feldkommandantur 752 | K.K. 733/FG | 23.1.42 |
| Feldkommandantur 752 | FG Trupp der F.K. 740 | 23.1.42 |
| Feldkommandantur 753 | FG Trupp a (mot) der F.K. 753 | ? |
| Feldkommandantur 753 | FG Trupp c (tmot) der F.K. 753 | 9.9.41 |
| Feldkommandantur 757 | F.K. 757 FG Trupp a (mot) | 11.12.40 |

| | | |
|---|---|---|
| Feldkommandantur 757 | FG Trupp c (tmot) 757 | 17.9.41 |
| Feldkommandantur 758 | FG Trupp d 895 | 21.9.40 |
| Feldkommandantur 758 | FG Trupp der F.K. 758 | 30.10.40 |
| Feldkommandantur 758 | FG Trupp a (mot) 902 | 9.1.42 |
| Feldkommandantur 774 | FG Trupp der F.K. 774 | 15.1.42 |
| Feldkommandantur 774 (Sich.Div. 444) | FG Trupp der F.K. 774 | 22.2.42 |
| Feldkommandantur 808 | FG Gruppe bei der F.K. 808 | 7.8.40 |
| Feldkommandantur 809 | F.K. V/809 FG Gruppe | 8.8.40 |
| Feldkommandantur 816 | F.K. (V)816 FG Gruppe | 8.8.40 |
| Feldkommandantur 817 | FG Trupp d 1124 | 12.5.44 |
| Feldkommandantur 1030 | FG Trupp d 1125 | 12.5.44 |
| Feldkommandantur 1034 | FG Trupp d 1126 | 12.5.44 |
| Feldkommandantur 1039 | FG Trupp d 1127 | 12.5.44 |
| Feldkommandantur 1040 | FG Trupp d 1128 | 12.5.44 |
| Feldkommandantur 1042 | FG Trupp d 1129 | 12.5.44 |
| Feldkommandantur Lillehammer | FG Trupp c (tmot) 606 | 15.9.43 |

**Festung (Fortress Headquarters)**

| | | |
|---|---|---|
| Festung Boulogne | FG Trupp (tmot) 1021 | 26.4.44 |
| Festung Brest | FG Trupp (tmot) 1025 | 26.4.44 |
| Festung Cherbourg | FG Trupp (tmot) 1023 | 26.4.44 |
| Festung Div. 41 | FG Trupp c (tmot) 141 | 17.11.43 |
| Festung Div. Kreta | FG Kp. (mot) 904 | 20.3.42 |
| Festung Duenkirchen | FG Trupp (tmot) 1020 | 26.4.44 |
| Festung Girondemuendung Nord | FG Trupp (tmot) 1033 | 26.4.44 |
| Festung Girondemuendung Sud | FG Trupp (tmot) 1034 | 26.4.44 |
| Festung Hoek v.Holland | FG Trupp (tmot) 1019 | 26.4.44 |
| Festung Kreta      2.Kp. | FG Abt (mot) 501 | 1.7.41 |
| Festung LeHavre | FG Trupp (tmot) 1022 | 26.4.44 |
| Festung Lorient | FG Trupp (tmot) 1026 | 26.4.44 |
| Festung St.Malo | FG Trupp (tmot) 1024 | 26.4.44 |
| Festung St.Nazaire | FG Trupp (tmot) 1027 | 26.4.44 |
| Festung Ymuiden | FG Trupp (tmot) 1018 | 26.4.44 |
| Festungskdtr.Thorn | FG Trupp 584 | 29.9.39 |
| Kommandant d.Festung Kreta | FG Trupp c (mot) 718 | 28.12.42 |
| Kommandant d.Festung Kreta | FG Trupp d (mot) 941 | 6.2.43 |
| Kommandant d.Festung Kreta | FG Trupp c (tmot) 985 | 6.2.43 |
| Kommandant d.Festung Kreta | FG Trupp a (mot) 904 | 23.2.43 |
| Kommandant d.Festung Kreta | FG Trupp a (mot) 133 | 2.2.44 |

**Grenz (Frontier Headquarters)**

| | | |
|---|---|---|
| Grenzkommandantur St. Wendel | FG Trupp (mot) 317 | 26.8.39 |
| Grz.Abschn.Kdo. 2 (Grenzschutz) | Grenzschutz-FG Trupp 2 | 26.8.39 |
| Grz.Abschn.Kdo.13 | FG Trupp (mot) 313 | 25.8.39 |
| Grz.Abschn.Kdo.13 | FG Trupp (mot) 313 | 6.10.39 |
| Grz.Abschn.Kdo.14 | FG Trupp (mot) 314 | 26.8.39 |
| Grz.Abschn.Kdo.30 | FG Trupp (mot) 330 | 23.9.39 |
| Grz.Abschn.Mitte | FG Trupp (mot) 314 | ? |

**Gruppe (Groupment Headquarters)**

| | | |
|---|---|---|
| Gruppe 21 | FG Trupp (mot) 571 | 13.3.40 |
| Gruppe Guderian | FG Trupp b (mot) 419 | 1.6.40 |
| Gruppe Schenckendorf | FG Trupp (mot) 313 | 5.9.39 |
| Gruppe von Kleist | Stab, FG Abt (mot) 501 | 7.3.40 |
| Gruppe von Kleist | 1.Kp. FG Abt (mot) 501 | 7.3.40 |
| Gruppe von Kleist | 2.Kp. FG Abt (mot) 501 | 7.3.40 |
| Gruppe von Kleist | 3.Kp. FG Abt (mot) 501 | 7.3.40 |

| | | |
|---|---|---|
| Gruppe von Kleist | FG Abt (mot) 685 (mit 2,3 Kp) | 20.3.40 |

**Heeresgruppe (Group of Armies Headquarters)**

| | | |
|---|---|---|
| H.Gr.A | O.K.II/706/FG | 18.3.40 |
| H.Gr.A | FG Gruppe der O.K.I(V) 505 | 29.6.40 |
| H.Gr.B | O.K. I/695/FG Trupp | 20.3.40 |
| H.Gr.B | F.K. 602/FG | 23.3.40 |
| H.Gr.C | FG Trupp 487 | 28.3.44 |
| H.Gr.C | FG Trupp 155 | 2.11.44 |
| H.Gr.C | O.K. I/552 FG | 30.8.39 |
| H.Gr.C | F.K. 560/FG | 30.8.39 |
| H.Gr.E | FG Trupp a (mot) 415 | 12.8.43 |
| H.Gr.E | FG Trupp a (mot) 422 | 12.8.43 |
| H.Gr.F | FG Gruppe/F.K. 1034 | 15.10.43 |
| H.Gr.F | FG Gruppe/F.K. 1028 | 27.10.43 |
| H.Gr.F | FG Gruppe/F.K. 1029 | 27.10.43 |
| H.Gr.F | FG Gruppe/F.K. 1030 | 27.10.43 |
| H.Gr.F | FG Gruppe/F.K. 1031 | 27.10.43 |
| H.Gr.F | FG Gruppe/F.K. 1032 | 27.10.43 |
| H.Gr.F | FG Gruppe/F.K. 1039 | 27.10.43 |
| H.Gr.F | FG Gruppe/F.K. 1040 | 27.10.43 |
| H.Gr.F | FG Gruppe/F.K. 1041 | 27.10.43 |
| H.Gr.F | FG Gruppe/F.K. 1042 | 27.10.43 |
| H.Gr.Mitte | FG Trupp d (tmot) 1045 | 4.1.45 |
| H.Gr.Sud | FG Trupp d (tmot) 1043 | 4.1.45 |
| H.Gr.Sud | FG Trupp d (tmot) 1044 | 4.1.45 |

**Kommandant (Commanding Officer)**

| | | |
|---|---|---|
| Kommandant v. Gross-Paris | FG Trupp c (tmot) 564 | 7.5.43 |
| Kommandant,Heeres Geb.Sud.Fr. | FG Trupp c (tmot) 983 | 2.8.42 |
| Kommandant,Heeres Geb.Sud.Fr. | FG Gruppe 992 | 14.12.42 |
| Kommandant,Heeres Geb.Sud.Fr. | FG Gruppe 995 | 14.12.42 |
| Kommandant,Heeres Geb.Sud.Fr. | FG Gruppe 994 | 21.12.42 |
| Kommandant,Heeres Geb.Sud.Fr. | FG Gruppe 987 | 22.12.42 |
| Kommandant,Heeres Geb.Sud.Fr. | FG Gruppe 988 | 22.12.42 |
| Kommandant,Heeres Geb.Sud.Fr. | FG Gruppe 983 | 28.12.42 |
| Kommandant,Heeres Geb.Sud.Fr. | FG Gruppe 711 | 31.12.42 |
| Kommandant,Heeres Geb.Sud.Fr. | FG Gruppe 577 | 1.1.43 |
| Kommandant,Heeres Geb.Sud.Fr. | FG Gruppe 730 | 1.1.43 |
| Kommandant,Heeres Geb.Sud.Fr. | FG Gruppe 739 | 1.1.43 |
| Kommandant,Heeres Geb.Sud.Fr. | FG Gruppe 659 | 1.3.43 |
| Kommandant,Heeres Geb.Sud.Fr. | FG Trupp d 964 | 1.3.43 |
| Kommandant,Heeres Geb.Sud.Fr. | FG Gruppe 732 | 1.3.43 |
| Kommandant,Heeres Geb.Sud.Fr. | FG Gruppe 734 | 1.3.43 |
| Kommandant,Heeres Geb.Sud.Fr. | FG Trupp d 967 | 1.3.43 |
| Kommandant,Heeres Geb.Sud.Fr. | FG Gruppe 747 | 1.3.43 |
| Kommandant,Heeres Geb.Sud.Fr. | FG Gruppe 761 | 1.3.43 |
| Kommandant,Heeres Geb.Sud.Fr. | FG Gruppe 792 | 1.3.43 |
| Kommandant,Heeres Geb.Sud.Fr. | FG Gruppe 798 | 1.3.43 |
| Kommandant,Heeres Geb.Sud.Fr. | FG Gruppe 800 | 1.3.43 |
| Kommandant,Heeres Geb.Sud.Fr. | FG Gruppe 802 | 1.3.43 |
| Kommandant,Heeres Geb.Sud.Fr. | FG Gruppe 806 | 1.3.43 |
| Kommandant,Heeres Geb.Sud.Fr. | FG Gruppe 989 | 1.3.43 |
| Kommandant,Heeres Geb.Sud.Fr. | FG Gruppe 990 | 1.3.43 |
| Kommandant,Heeres Geb.Sud.Fr. | FG Trupp d 986 | 1.3.43 |
| Kommandant,Heeres Geb.Sud.Fr. | FG Gruppe 993 | 1.3.43 |

| | | |
|---|---|---|
| Kommandant,Heeres Geb.Sud.Fr. | FG Trupp d 993 | 1.3.43 |
| Kommandant,Heeres Geb.Sud.Fr. | FG Gruppe 996 | 1.3.43 |
| Kommandant,Heeres Geb.Sud.Fr. | FG Gruppe 997 | 1.3.43 |
| Kommandant,Heeres Geb.Sud.Fr. | FG Trupp d 986 | 1.3.43 |
| Kommandant,Heeres Geb.Sud.Fr. | FG Trupp 564 | 11.3.43 |
| Kommandant,Heeres Geb.Sud.Fr. | FG Trupp c (tmot) 932 | 23.3.43 |
| Kommandant,Heeres Geb.Sud.Fr. | FG Trupp d 958 | 23.3.43 |
| Kommandant,Heeres Geb.Sud.Fr. | FG Trupp d 961 | 23.3.43 |
| Kommandant,Heeres Geb.Sud.Fr. | FG Trupp d 962 | 23.3.43 |
| Kommandant,Heeres Geb.Sud.Fr. | FG Trupp d 963 | 23.3.43 |
| Kommandant,Heeres Geb.Sud.Fr. | FG Trupp d 965 | 23.3.43 |
| Kommandant,Heeres Geb.Sud.Fr. | FG Trupp d 966 | 23.3.43 |
| Kommandant,Heeres Geb.Sud.Fr. | FG Trupp d 968 | 23.3.43 |
| Kommandant,Heeres Geb.Sud.Fr. | FG Trupp d 969 | 23.3.43 |
| Kommandant,Heeres Geb.Sud.Fr. | FG Trupp d 970 | 23.3.43 |
| Kommandant,Heeres Geb.Sud.Fr. | FG Trupp d 971 | 23.3.43 |
| Kommandant,Heeres Geb.Sud.Fr. | FG Trupp d 972 | 23.3.43 |
| Kommandant,Heeres Geb.Sud.Fr. | FG Trupp d 973 | 23.3.43 |
| Kommandant,Heeres Geb.Sud.Fr. | FG Trupp d 974 | 23.3.43 |
| Kommandant,Heeres Geb.Sud.Fr. | FG Trupp d 975 | 23.3.43 |
| Kommandant,Heeres Geb.Sud.Fr. | FG Trupp d 976 | 23.3.43 |
| Kommandant,Heeres Geb.Sud.Fr. | FG Trupp d 977 | 23.3.43 |
| Kommandant,Heeres Geb.Sud.Fr. | FG Trupp d 978 | 23.3.43 |
| Kommandant,Heeres Geb.Sud.Fr. | FG Trupp d 979 | 23.3.43 |
| Kommandant,Heeres Geb.SudFr. | FG Trupp d 980 | 23.3.43 |
| Kommandant,Heeres Geb.Sud.Fr. | FG Trupp a (mot) 987 | 23.3.43 |
| Kommandant,Heeres Geb.Sud.Fr. | FG Trupp a 988 | 23.3.43 |
| Kommandant,Heeres Geb.Sud.Fr. | FG Trupp d 991 | 23.3.43 |
| Kommandant,Heeres Geb.Sud.Fr. | FG Trupp d 992 | 23.3.43 |
| Kommandant,Heeres Geb.Sud.Fr. | FG Trupp d 994 | 23.3.43 |
| Kommandant,Heeres Geb.Sud.Fr. | FG Trupp 983 | 23.3.43 |
| Kommandant,Heeres Geb.Sud.Fr. | FG Trupp d 995 | 23.3.43 |
| Kommandant,Heeres Geb.Sud.Fr. | FG Trupp d 694 | 16.9.43 |
| Kommandant,Heeres Geb.Sud.Fr. | FG Trupp d 695 | 16.9.43 |
| Kommandant,Heeres Geb.Sud.Fr. | FG Trupp b (mot) 689 | 10.7.44 |
| Kommandant,Heeres Geb.Sud.Fr. | FG Trupp b (mot) 690 | 10.7.44 |

**Kommando (Headquarters)**

| | | |
|---|---|---|
| Kommando Boehmen-Maehren | FG Trupp 1151 | 21.12.44 |
| Kommando Boehmen-Maehren | FG Trupp 1049 | 17.1.45 |
| Kommando L.P. Danzig | FG Trupp der L.P. Danzig | 26.8.39 |
| Kommando Sardinien | FG Trupp a (mot) Kdo.Sardinien | 27.5.43 |
| Kommando Sardinien | FG Trupp a (mot) Kdo.Sardinien | 15.6.43 |
| Kommando Sardinien | FG Trupp 652 | 11.12.43 |
| Kommando Sizilien | FG Trupp a (mot) Kdo.Sizilien | 27.5.43 |

**Korueck (Commanding Officer Rear Area Zone)**

| | | |
|---|---|---|
| Korueck 9 | O.K.II/744 FG Gruppe | 20.5.40 |
| Korueck 501 | Stab, FG Abt (mot) 501 | 16.8.39 |
| Korueck 501 | 1.Kp. FG Abt (mot) 501 | 16.8.39 |
| Korueck 501 | 2.Kp. FG Abt (mot) 501 | 16.8.39 |
| Korueck 501 | 3.Kp. FG Abt (mot) 501 | 16.8.39 |
| Korueck 501 | O.K. I/501 FG | 25.8.39 |
| Korueck 525 | FG Trupp c (tmot) 462 | 18.1.43 |
| Korueck 530 | O.K. I/533 FG | 26.8.39 |
| Korueck 540 | O.K. I/542 FG | 26.8.39 |

| | | |
|---|---|---|
| Korueck 540 | O.K. I/544 FG | 26.8.39 |
| Korueck 540 | FG Abt (mot) 683 | 28.8.39 |
| Korueck 550 | Stab, FG Abt 551 | 26.8.39 |
| Korueck 550 | O.K.II/558 FG | 11.9.39 |
| Korueck 550 | O.K. I/621 FG | 20.6.40 |
| Korueck 550 | O.K. I/622 FG | 20.6.40 |
| Korueck 550 | Stab, FG Abt 551 | 14.8.40 |
| Korueck 560 | F.K. V/809 FG Gruppe | 21.2.41 |
| Korueck 560 | Stab, FG Abt (mot) 501 | 26.2.41 |
| Korueck 560 | 1.Kp. FG Abt (mot) 501 | 26.2.41 |
| Korueck 560 | 2.Kp. FG Abt (mot) 501 | 26.2.41 |
| Korueck 560 | 3.Kp. FG Abt (mot) 501 | 26.2.41 |
| Korueck 580 | 1.Kp. Ub. FG Abt 581 | 2.8.39 |
| Korueck 580 | 2.Kp. Ub. FG Abt 581 | 2.8.39 |
| Korueck 580 | 3.Kp. Ub. FG Abt 581 | 2.8.39 |
| Korueck 580 | O.K.II/586 | 2.8.39 |
| Korueck 580 | 1.Kp. FG Abt (mot) 581 | 26.8.39 |
| Korueck 580 | 2.Kp. FG Abt (mot) 581 | 26.8.39 |
| Korueck 580 | 3.Kp. FG Abt (mot) 581 | 26.8.39 |
| Korueck 580 | O.K. I/583 FG | 26.8.39 |
| Korueck 580 | FG Abt (mot) 685 (mit 1,2,3 Kp) | 21.11.39 |
| Korueck 580 | Stab, FG Abt 551 | 4.1.41 |
| Korueck 582 | O.K. I/533 FG | 20.9.39 |
| Korueck 582 | O.K.II/745 FG | 20.5.40 |
| Korueck 582 | O.K. I/728 FG | 8.6.40 |
| Korueck 583 | O.K. I/634 FG | 15.10.39 |
| Korueck 583 | O.K. I/641 FG | 27.10.39 |
| Korueck 583 | FG Abt (mot) 685 (mit 1,2,3 Kp) | 17.11.39 |
| Korueck 583 | F.K. 568/FG | 15.12.39 |
| Korueck 583 | O.K. I/533 FG | 2.2.40 |
| Korueck 583 | O.K. I/641 FG | 27.5.40 |
| Korueck 585 | O.K. I/544 FG | 28.10.39 |
| Korueck 585 | O.K. I/542 FG | 29.10.39 |
| Korueck 585 | O.K. I/542 FG | 3.2.40 |
| Korueck 585, A.O.K. 6 | FG Trupp der F.K. 541 | 30.6.40 |
| Korueck 588  Bordeaux | FG Trupp 732 der K.K. 732 | 11.11.42 |
| Korueck 588  Bordeaux | FG Trupp der O.K. 73 | 12.11.42 |
| Korueck 590 | F.K. 590/FG | 26.8.39 |
| Korueck 590 | O.K. I/594 FG | 26.8.39 |
| Korueck 590 | O.K.II/FG Trupp 595 | 26.8.39 |
| Korueck 590 | O.K.II/592 FG | 28.8.39 |
| Korueck 590 | O.K.II/592 FG | 15.3.40 |
| Korueck 590 | O.K. I/594 FG | 11.6.40 |
| Korueck Sued Polen | FG Abt (mot) 685 (mit 1,2,3 Kp) | 30.9.39 |
| Korueck der Gruppe 21 | FG Abt. Korueck der Gruppe 21 | 15.6.40 |

**Kreiskommandantur (Area Headquarters)**

| | | |
|---|---|---|
| Kreiskommandantur 505 (La Rochelle) | FG Trupp d 796 | 15.1.42 |
| Kreiskommandantur 533 | FG Trupp 543 | 15.11.44 |
| Kreiskommandantur 563 | FG Trupp 888 | 15.1.42 |
| Kreiskommandantur 622 | FG Trupp 711 | 8.1.41 |
| Kreiskommandantur 622 | FG Trupp 721 | 24.7.42 |
| Kreiskommandantur 645 | FG Trupp 797 | 6.1.42 |
| Kreiskommandantur 703 | FG Trupp d 53 | 17.8.41 |
| Kreiskommandantur 703 | FG Trupp d 814 | 27.10.41 |

| | | |
|---|---|---|
| Kreiskommandantur 706 | FG Trupp 795 | 15.1.42 |
| Kreiskommandantur 711 | FG Trupp 711 | 1.12.41 |
| Kreiskommandantur 734 | FG Trupp 765 | 20.6.42 |
| Kreiskommandantur 738 | FG Trupp d 738 | 15.10.40 |
| Kreiskommandantur 743 | FG Trupp d (mot) 743 | 1.4.41 |
| Kreiskommandantur 747 | FG Trupp 780 | 7.1.42 |
| Kreiskommandantur 759 | K.K. 759 FG Trupp | 8.7.40 |
| Kreiskommandantur 767 (Schlesien) | K.K. I/767 FG | 14.6.40 |
| Kreiskommandantur 773 | FG Trupp d (mot) 743 | 10.1.42 |
| Kreiskommandantur 780 | FG Trupp 780 | 7.9.40 |
| Kreiskommandantur 792 | FG Trupp 792 | 3.8.40 |
| Kreiskommandantur 798 | FG Trupp 765 | ? |
| Kreiskommandantur 801 | K.K. 801 FG | 28.8.40 |
| Kreiskommandantur 802 | O.K. I (V)/802 FG Gruppe | 10.9.40 |
| Kreiskommandantur 832 | FG Trupp d 864 | 15.11.41 |
| Kreiskommandantur 867 | K.K. I (V)/867 FG Gruppe | 5.7.41 |
| Kreiskommandantur 887 | FG Trupp der K.K.887 | 11.9.40 |
| Kreiskommandantur 887 | FG Trupp 887 | 1.12.41 |
| Kreiskommandantur 889 | K.K. I/889 FG | 10.9.40 |
| Kreiskommandantur 890 | FG Trupp der K.K. 890 | 11.9.40 |
| Kreiskommandantur 894 | FG Trupp c (tmot) 589 | 20.3.42 |
| Kreiskommandantur 895 | FG Trupp d 738 | 10.1.42 |
| Kreiskommandantur 896 (Paris) | FG Trupp d der K.K. 896 | 31.10.40 |

**Militaerkommandantur (Military Headquarters)**

| | | |
|---|---|---|
| Mil.Kdtr. 1006 Ferrara | FG Trupp d 526 | 17.1.44 |

**Chef der Militaerverwaltungs (Chief of Military Administration)**

| | | |
|---|---|---|
| Chef der Mil.Verw.,Bez.B | FG Trupp 582 der K.K.582 | 10.9.40 |
| Chef der Mil.Verw.,Bez.B | FG Trupp 547 der K.K.547 | 28.9.40 |
| Chef der Mil.Verw.,Bez.B | FG Trupp 750 der F.K.750 | 21.6.41 |
| Chef der Mil.Verw.,Bez.B | FG Trupp 511 | 15.11.41 |
| Chef der Mil.Verw.,Bez.B | FG Trupp 547 der K.K.582 | 15.1.42 |
| Chef der Mil.Verw.,Bez.Paris | FG Trupp 584 | 24.11.40 |
| Chef der Mil.Verw.i.Fr. | O.K. I/533 FG | 1.7.40 |
| Chef der Mil.Verw.i.Fr. | O.K.II/744 FG Gruppe | 1.7.40 |
| Chef der Mil.Verw.i.Fr. | O.K. I/542 FG | 2.7.40 |
| Chef der Mil.Verw.i.Fr. | O.K. I/645 FG | 12.7.40 |
| Chef der Mil.Verw.i.Fr. | FG Abt (mot) 683 | 8.8.40 |
| Chef der Mil.Verw.i.Fr. | FG Trupp der K.K.543 | 7.9.40 |
| Chef der Mil.Verw.i.Fr. (Paris) | Stab, FG Abt (mot) 501 | 9.7.40 |
| Chef der Mil.Verw.i.Fr. (Paris) | 1.Kp. FG Abt (mot) 501 | 9.7.40 |
| Chef der Mil.Verw.i.Fr. (Paris) | 2.Kp. FG Abt (mot) 501 | 9.7.40 |
| Chef der Mil.Verw.i.Fr. (Paris) | 3.Kp. FG Abt (mot) 501 | 2.8.40 |
| Chef der Mil.Verw.i.Fr.,Bez.A | O.K. I(V) 800 FG | 10.8.40 |
| Chef der Mil.Verw.i.Fr.,Bez.A | O.K. I/832 FG Gruppe | 20.8.40 |
| Chef der Mil.Verw.i.Fr.,Bez.A | K.K. 645/FG | 10.9.40 |
| Chef der Mil.Verw.i.Fr.,Bez.A | FG Trupp 645 | 15.11.41 |
| Chef der Mil.Verw.i.Fr.,Bez.A | FG Trupp 800 | 26.11.41 |
| Chef der Mil.Verw.i.Fr.,Bez.B | FG Trupp 794 der K.K. 794 | 28.9.40 |
| Chef der Mil.Verw.i.Fr.,Bez.B | FG Trupp 794 der K.K. 582 | 15.1.42 |
| Chef der Mil.Verw.i.Fr.,Bez.C | O.K. I/634 FG | 1.7.40 |
| Chef der Mil.Verw.i.Fr.,Bez.C | O.K. I/776 FG Trupp | 9.7.40 |
| Chef der Mil.Verw.i.Fr.,Bez.C | K.K. 731/FG Gruppe | 31.10.40 |
| Chef der Mil.Verw.i.Fr.,Bez.C | O.K. I/832 FG Gruppe | 21.11.40 |
| Chef der Mil.Verw.i.Fr.,Bez.C | FG Trupp 634 der K.K. 634 | 17.8.41 |

| | | |
|---|---|---|
| Chef der Mil.Verw.i.Fr.,Bez.C | FG Trupp 634 | 15.11.41 |
| Chef der Mil.Verw.i.Fr.,Bez.C(Bourges) | O.K. I/731 FG Gruppe | 1.7.40 |
| Chef der Mil.Verw.i.Fr.,Bez.C(Vierzon) | O.K. I/731 FG Gruppe | 9.9.40 |
| Chef.der Mil.Verw.Wesens (Dijon) | O.K. I/641 FG | 1.7.40 |

**Militaerverwaltungs (Military Administration)**

| | | |
|---|---|---|
| Mil.Verw.Bez.A | FG Gruppe der K.K.527 | 19.6.40 |
| Mil.Verw.Bez.A | F.K. 610/V/FG Gruppe | 31.10.40 |
| Mil.Verw.Bez.A | FG Trupp der K.K.527 | 17.8.41 |
| Mil.Verw.Bez.A | FG Trupp 527 K.K.797 | 15.11.41 |
| Mil.Verw.Bez.A./Nordwestfr. | FG Trupp 583 | 9.9.41 |
| Mil.Verw.Bez.B | F.K. 605/FG Trupp c (tmot) | 17.8.41 |
| Mil.Verw.Bez.B | FG Trupp 528 | 15.11.41 |
| Mil.Verw.Bez.B | FG Trupp 539 | 15.1.42 |
| Mil.Verw.Bez.B | FG Trupp 540 | 15.1.42 |
| Mil.Verw.Bez.B./Sudwestfr. | K.K. 790 FG | 31.7.40 |
| Mil.Verw.Bez.B./Sudwestfr. | K.K. 790 FG Trupp d | 20.9.40 |
| Mil.Verw.Bez.B./Sudwestfr. | FG Trupp c (tmot) 657 | 15.1.42 |
| Mil.Verw.Bez.B./Sudwestfr. | FG Trupp a (mot) 524 | 15.1.42 |
| Mil.Verw.Bez.B./Sudwestfr.Angers | FG Trupp 659 der K.K. 659 | 15.1.42 |
| Mil.Verw.Bez.Bordeaux | FG Trupp der F.K. 541 | 20.9.40 |
| Mil.Verw.Bez.Bordeaux | FG Trupp 505 | 15.1.41 |
| Mil.Verw.Bez.Bordeaux | K.K. I/564 FG | 21.8.41 |
| Mil.Verw.Bez.Bordeaux | F.K. 605/FG Trupp c (tmot) | 21.8.41 |
| Mil.Verw.Bez.Bordeaux | K.K. 655/FG | 21.8.41 |
| Mil.Verw.Bez.Bordeaux | FG Trupp a (mot) 524 | 15.11.41 |
| Mil.Verw.Bez.Bordeaux | FG Trupp 564 | 15.11.41 |
| Mil.Verw.Bez.Bordeaux | FG Trupp c (tmot) 615 | 15.11.41 |
| Mil.Verw.Bez.Bordeaux | FG Trupp 655 | 15.11.41 |
| Mil.Verw.Bez.C | O.K. I/624 FG | 20.7.40 |
| Mil.Verw.Bez.C | O.K. I/553 FG | 24.7.40 |
| Mil.Verw.Bez.C | K.K. 553/FG | 10.9.40 |
| Mil.Verw.Bez.C | K.K. 624/FG | 10.9.40 |
| Mil.Verw.Bez.C | FG Trupp c (tmot) der F.K.560 | 7.10.41 |
| Mil.Verw.Bez.C | FG Trupp 553 | 15.11.41 |
| Mil.Verw.Bez.C | FG Trupp 566 | 15.11.41 |
| Mil.Verw.Bez.C | FG Trupp 624 | 15.11.41 |
| Mil.Verw.Bez.Paris | FG Trupp der K.K. 761 | 17.6.40 |
| Mil.Verw.i.Fr. | K.K. 533/FG | 10.9.40 |
| Mil.Verw.i.Fr. | K.K.II/744 FG Gruppe | 10.9.40 |
| Mil.Verw.i.Fr.,Mil.Verw.Bez.A | F.K. 722/Gendarmerie | 18.6.40 |
| Mil.Verw.i.Fr.,Mil.Verw.Bez.A | O.K.II/586 FG | 1.7.40 |
| Mil.Verw.i.Fr.,Mil.Verw.Bez.A | O.K.II/706 FG | 3.7.40 |
| Mil.Verw.i.Fr.,Mil.Verw.Bez.A | O.K.II/577 FG | 7.7.40 |
| Mil.Verw.i.Fr.,Mil.Verw.Bez.A | F.K. 602/FG | 15.7.40 |
| Mil.Verw.i.Fr.,Mil.Verw.Bez.A | O.K. I/729 FG | 30.7.40 |
| Mil.Verw.i.Fr.,Mil.Verw.Bez.A | K.K. 741 FG | 30.7.40 |
| Mil.Verw.i.Fr.,Mil.Verw.Bez.A | O.K. 797 FG | 5.8.40 |
| Mil.Verw.i.Fr.,Mil.Verw.Bez.A | F.K. V/809 FG Gruppe | 24.8.40 |
| Mil.Verw.i.Fr.,Mil.Verw.Bez.A | O.K. I(V) 789 FG | 2.9.40 |
| Mil.Verw.i.Fr.,Mil.Verw.Bez.A | K.K. 567/FG | 10..40 |
| Mil.Verw.i.Fr.,Mil.Verw.Bez.A | K.K. 577/FG | 10.9.40 |
| Mil.Verw.i.Fr.,Mil.Verw.Bez.A | K.K. 586/FG | 10.9.40 |
| Mil.Verw.i.Fr.,Mil.Verw.Bez.A | K.K. 729/FG | 10.9.40 |
| Mil.Verw.i.Fr.,Mil.Verw.Bez.A | K.K. 742 FG | 10.9.40 |

| | | |
|---|---|---|
| Mil.Verw.i.Fr.,Mil.Verw.Bez.A | K.K. 789 FG | 10.9.40 |
| Mil.Verw.i.Fr.,Mil.Verw.Bez.A | K.K. 797 FG | 10.9.40 |
| Mil.Verw.i.Fr.,Mil.Verw.Bez.A | K.K. 882/FG Trupp | 19.9.40 |
| Mil.Verw.i.Fr.,Mil.Verw.Bez.A | FG Gruppe der K.K.544 | 20.9.40 |
| Mil.Verw.i.Fr.,Mil.Verw.Bez.A | K.K. 731/FG Gruppe | 20.9.40 |
| Mil.Verw.i.Fr.,Mil.Verw.Bez.A | F.K. 776 FG | 20.9.40 |
| Mil.Verw.i.Fr.,Mil.Verw.Bez.A | K.K. 884 FG | 7.10.40 |
| Mil.Verw.i.Fr.,Mil.Verw.Bez.A | FG Trupp a (mot) 223 | 30.10.40 |
| Mil.Verw.i.Fr.,Mil.Verw.Bez.A | FG Trupp d 776 | 31.10.40 |
| Mil.Verw.i.Fr.,Mil.Verw.Bez.A | FG Trupp d (mot) der K.K.884 | 15.11.40 |
| Mil.Verw.i.Fr.,Mil.Verw.Bez.A | FG Trupp der K.K.544 | 3.12.40 |
| Mil.Verw.i.Fr.,Mil.Verw.Bez.A | FG Trupp 884 | 17.8.41 |
| Mil.Verw.i.Fr.,Mil.Verw.Bez.A | FG Trupp d 804 | 17.9.41 |
| Mil.Verw.i.Fr.,Mil.Verw.Bez.A | FG Trupp c (tmot) 579 | 22.9.41 |
| Mil.Verw.i.Fr.,Mil.Verw.Bez.A | FG Trupp 567 | 15.11.41 |
| Mil.Verw.i.Fr.,Mil.Verw.Bez.A | FG Trupp 577 | 15.11.41 |
| Mil.Verw.i.Fr.,Mil.Verw.Bez.A | FG Trupp 515 | 15.11.41 |
| Mil.Verw.i.Fr.,Mil.Verw.Bez.A | FG Trupp 722 | 15.11.41 |
| Mil.Verw.i.Fr.,Mil.Verw.Bez.A | FG Trupp 741 | 15.11.41 |
| Mil.Verw.i.Fr.,Mil.Verw.Bez.A | FG Trupp der K.K. 742 | 15.11.41 |
| Mil.Verw.i.Fr.,Mil.Verw.Bez.A | FG Trupp 789 | 15.11.41 |
| Mil.Verw.i.Fr.,Mil.Verw.Bez.A | FG Trupp 797 | 15.11.41 |
| Mil.Verw.i.Fr.,Mil.Verw.Bez.A | FG Trupp 882 | 15.11.41 |
| Mil.Verw.i.Fr.,Mil.Verw.Bez.A | FG Trupp 544 | 1.12.41 |
| Mil.Verw.i.Fr.,Mil.Verw.Bez.A | FG Trupp c (mot) 589 | 1.12.41 |
| Mil.Verw.i.Fr.,Mil.Verw.Bez.A | FG Trupp 866 | 1.12.41 |
| Mil.Verw.i.Fr.,Mil.Verw.Bez.A | FG Trupp 742 der K.K. 894 | 10.1.42 |
| Mil.Verw.i.Fr.,Mil.Verw.Bez.A | FG Trupp 731 der K.K. 776 | 15.1.42 |
| Mil.Verw.i.Fr.,Mil.Verw.Bez.A | FG Trupp a (mot) 751 | 14.3.42 |
| Mil.Verw.i.Fr.,Mil.Verw.Bez.B | F.K. 677/FG | 2.6.40 |
| Mil.Verw.i.Fr.,Mil.Verw.Bez.B | O.K. I/564 FG | 1.7.40 |
| Mil.Verw.i.Fr.,Mil.Verw.Bez.B | O.K. I/730 FG | 3.7.40 |
| Mil.Verw.i.Fr.,Mil.Verw.Bez.B | O.K. I/734 FG | 3.7.40 |
| Mil.Verw.i.Fr.,Mil.Verw.Bez.B | F.K. 540/FG | 9.7.40 |
| Mil.Verw.i.Fr.,Mil.Verw.Bez.B | O.K. I/779 FG | 9.7.40 |
| Mil.Verw.i. Fr.,Mil.Verw. Bez. B  Angers | O.K. I/732 FG Trupp | 12.7.40 |
| Mil.Verw.i.Fr.,Mil.Verw.Bez.B | O.K.II/597 FG | 24.7.40 |
| Mil.Verw.i.Fr.,Mil.Verw.Bez.B | O.K. I/607 FG | 30.7.40 |
| Mil.Verw.i.Fr.,Mil.Verw.Bez.B | O.K.II/609 FG | 30.7.40 |
| Mil.Verw.i.Fr.,Mil.Verw.Bez.B | F.K. 605/FG | 30.7.40 |
| Mil.Verw.i.Fr.,Mil.Verw.Bez.B | O.K. I/651 FG | 30.7.40 |
| Mil.Verw.i.Fr.,Mil.Verw.Bez.B | O.K.II/655/FG | 30.7.40 |
| Mil.Verw.i.Fr.,Mil.Verw.Bez.B | O.K.II/665/FG | 30.7.40 |
| Mil.Verw.i.Fr.,Mil.Verw.Bez.B | O.K. I/735 FG | 30.7.40 |
| Mil.Verw.i.Fr.,Mil.Verw.Bez.B | O.K.II/736 FG | 30.7.40 |
| Mil.Verw.i.Fr.,Mil.Verw.Bez.B | O.K. I/777 FG | 30.7.40 |
| Mil.Verw.i.Fr.,Mil.Verw.Bez.B | O.K.II/739 FG Gruppe | 18.8.40 |
| Mil.Verw.i.Fr.,Mil.Verw.Bez.B | O.K. I(V) 796 FG | 25.8.40 |
| Mil.Verw.i.Fr.,Mil.Verw.Bez.B | O.K. I (V)/803 FG | 1.9.40 |
| Mil.Verw.i.Fr.,Mil.Verw.Bez.B | O.K.II/FG Trupp 595 | 6.9.40 |
| Mil.Verw.i.Fr.,Mil.Verw.Bez.B | O.K. I/793 FG | 8.9.40 |
| Mil.Verw.i.Fr.,Mil.VerwBez.B | K.K. 595/FG | 10.9.40 |
| Mil.Verw.i.Fr.,Mil.Verw.Bez.B | K.K. 597/FG | 10.9.40 |
| Mil.Verw.i.Fr.,Mil.Verw.Bez.B | K.K. I/564 FG | 10.9.40 |

| | | |
|---|---|---|
| Mil.Verw.i.Fr.,Mil.Verw.Bez.B | K.K. 607/FG | 10.9.40 |
| Mil.Verw.i.Fr.,Mil.Verw.Bez.B | K.K. 609 FG | 10.9.40 |
| Mil.Verw.i.Fr.,Mil.Verw.Bez.B | FG Gruppe der O.K.I(V) in K.K. 505 | 10.9.40 |
| Mil.Verw.i.Fr.,Mil.Verw.Bez.B | K.K. 651/FG | 10.9.40 |
| Mil.Verw.i.Fr.,Mil.Verw.Bez.B | K.K. 655/FG | 10.9.40 |
| Mil.Verw.i.Fr.,Mil.Verw.Bez.B | K.K. 665/FG | 10.9.40 |
| Mil.Verw.i.Fr.,Mil.Verw.Bez.B | K.K. I/730 FG | 10.9.40 |
| Mil.Verw.i.Fr.,Mil.Verw.Bez.B | K.K. I/734 FG | 10.9.40 |
| Mil.Verw.i.Fr.,Mil.Verw.Bez.B | K.K. I/735 FG | 10.9.40 |
| Mil.Verw.i.Fr.,Mil.Verw.Bez.B | K.K. 736 FG | 10.9.40 |
| Mil.Verw.i.Fr.,Mil.Verw.Bez.B | K.K. 739 FG | 10.9.40 |
| Mil.Verw.i.Fr.,Mil.Verw.Bez.B | K.K. 793 FG | 10.9.40 |
| Mil.Verw.i.Fr.,Mil.Verw.Bez.B | K.K. 803 FG | 10.9.40 |
| Mil.Verw.i.Fr.,Mil.Verw.Bez.B | K.K. 768 FG | 10.9.40 |
| Mil.Verw.i.Fr.,Mil.Verw.Bez.B | K.K. I/777 FG | 10.9.40 |
| Mil.Verw.i.Fr.,Mil.Verw.Bez.B | K.K. 779 FG | 10.9.40 |
| Mil.Verw.i.Fr.,Mil.Verw.Bez.B | K.K. 586/FG | 20.9.40 |
| Mil.Verw.i.Fr., Mil.Verw.Bez. B  Angers | K.K. V/732 FG | 20.9.40 |
| Mil.Verw.i.Fr.,Mil.Verw.Bez.B | F.K. V/809 FG Gruppe | 20.9.40 |
| Mil.Verw.i.Fr.,Mil.Verw.Bez.B | FG Trupp a (mot) 211 | 21.10.40 |
| Mil.Verw.i.Fr.,Mil.Verw.Bez.B | FG Trupp a (mot) 677 | 31.10.40 |
| Mil.Verw.i.Fr.,Mil.Verw.Bez.B | K.K. 735 FG | 4.11.40 |
| Mil.Verw.i.Fr.,Mil.Verw.Bez.B  Angers | FG Trupp 518 | 1.12.40 |
| Mil.Verw.i.Fr.,Mil.Verw.Bez.B | FG Trupp a (mot) 210 | 11.6.41 |
| Mil.Verw.i.Fr.,Mil.Verw.Bez.B | FG Trupp 748 | 17.8.41 |
| Mil.Verw.i.Fr.,Mil.Verw.Bez.B | FG Trupp 735 | 4.11.41 |
| Mil.Verw.i.Fr.,Mil.Verw.Bez.B | FG Trupp 607 | 15.11.41 |
| Mil.Verw.i.Fr.,Mil.Verw.Bez.B | FG Trupp 609 | 15.11.41 |
| Mil.Verw.i.Fr.,Mil.Verw.Bez.B | FG Trupp 586 | 15.11.41 |
| Mil.Verw.i.Fr.,Mil.Verw.Bez.B | FG Trupp 635 | 15.11.41 |
| Mil.Verw.i.Fr.,Mil.Verw.Bez.B | FG Trupp 665 | 15.11.41 |
| Mil.Verw.i.Fr.,Mil.Verw.Bez.B | FG Trupp 729 | 15.11.41 |
| Mil.Verw.i.Fr.,Mil.Verw.Bez.B | FG Trupp 735 | 15.11.41 |
| Mil.Verw.i.Fr.,Mil.Verw.Bez.B | FG Trupp 793 | 15.11.41 |
| Mil.Verw.i.Fr.,Mil.Verw.Bez.B | FG Trupp d 796 | 15.11.41 |
| Mil.Verw.i.Fr.,Mil.Verw.Bez.B | FG Trupp 768 | 15.11.41 |
| Mil.Verw.i.Fr.,Mil.Verw.Bez.B  Angers | FG Trupp 877 | 27.11.41 |
| Mil.Verw.i.Fr.,Mil.Verw.Bez.B | FG Trupp d 597 | 15.1.42 |
| Mil.Verw.i.Fr.,Mil.Verw.Bez.B | FG Trupp 564 | 15.1.42 |
| Mil.Verw.i.Fr.,Mil.Verw.Bez.B | FG Trupp 651 | 15.1.42 |
| Mil.Verw.i.Fr.,Mil.Verw.Bez.B | FG Trupp 655 | 15.1.42 |
| Mil.Verw.i.Fr.,Mil.Verw.Bez.B | FG Trupp c (mot) 677 | 15.1.42 |
| Mil.Verw.i.Fr.,Mil.Verw.Bez.B | FG Trupp 730 | 15.1.42 |
| Mil.Verw.i.Fr.,Mil.Verw.Bez.B  Angers | FG Trupp 732 der K.K. 732 | 15.1.42 |
| Mil.Verw.i.Fr.,Mil.Verw.Bez.B | FG Trupp 734 | 15.1.42 |
| Mil.Verw.i.Fr.,Mil.Verw.Bez.B | FG Trupp 736 | 15.1.42 |
| Mil.Verw.i.Fr.,Mil.Verw.Bez.B | FG Trupp d 739 | 15.1.42 |
| Mil.Verw.i.Fr.,Mil.Verw.Bez.B | FG Trupp 860 | 15.1.42 |
| Mil.Verw.i.Fr.,Mil.Verw.Bez.B | FG Trupp 764 | 15.1.42 |
| Mil.Verw.i.Fr.,Mil.Verw.Bez.B | FG Trupp 777 | 15.1.42 |
| Mil.Verw.i.Fr.,Mil.Verw.Bez.B | FG Trupp 779 | 15.1.42 |
| Mil.Verw.i.Fr.,Mil.Verw.Bez.B | FG Trupp a (mot) 510 | 28.11.42 |
| Mil.Verw.i.Fr.,Mil.Verw.Bez.Bordeaux | K.K. 764 FG | 10.9.40 |
| Mil.Verw.i.Fr.,Mil.Verw.Bez.Bordeaux | F.K. 540 FG | 20.9.40 |

| | | |
|---|---|---|
| Mil.Verw.i.Fr.,Mil.Verw.Bez.Bordeaux | K.K. V/732 FG | 20.9.40 |
| Mil.Verw.i.Fr.,Mil.Verw.Bez.Bordeaux | K.K. I/734 FG | 20.9.40 |
| Mil.Verw.i.Fr.,Mil.Verw.Bez.Bordeaux | K.K. I/777 FG | 20.9.40 |
| Mil.Verw.i.Fr.,Mil.Verw.Bez.Bordeaux | K.K. 779 FG | 20.9.40 |
| Mil.Verw.i.Fr.,Mil.Verw.Bez.Bordeaux | FG Trupp der K.K. 659 | 30.9.40 |
| Mil.Verw.i.Fr.,Mil.Verw.Bez.Bordeaux | K.K. I/730 FG | 11.10.40 |
| Mil.Verw.i.Fr.,Mil.Verw.Bez.Bordeaux | O.K. I/764 FG | 26.10.40 |
| Mil.Verw.i.Fr.,Mil.Verw.Bez.Bordeaux | FG Trupp c (tmot) der K.K. 657 | 17.8.41 |
| Mil.Verw.i.Fr.,Mil.Verw.Bez.Bordeaux | K.K. 597/FG | 21.8.41 |
| Mil.Verw.i.Fr.,Mil.Verw.Bez.Bordeaux | K.K. 651/FG | 21.8.41 |
| Mil.Verw.i.Fr.,Mil.Verw.Bez.Bordeaux | FG Trupp a (mot) 677 | 21.8.41 |
| Mil.Verw.i.Fr.,Mil.Verw.Bez.Bordeaux | K.K. 736 FG | 21.8.41 |
| Mil.Verw.i.Fr.,Mil.Verw.Bez.Bordeaux | K.K. 739 FG | 21.8.41 |
| Mil.Verw.i.Fr.,Mil.Verw.Bez.Bordeaux | K.K. 803 FG | 21.8.41 |
| Mil.Verw.i.Fr.,Mil.Verw.Bez.Bordeaux | FG Trupp c (tmot) 677 | 1.10.41 |
| Mil.Verw.i.Fr.,Mil.Verw.Bez.Bordeaux | FG Trupp II der F.K. 540 | 10.10.41 |
| Mil.Verw.i.Fr.,Mil.Verw.Bez.Bordeaux | FG Trupp 540 | 15.11.41 |
| Mil.Verw.i.Fr.,Mil.Verw.Bez.Bordeaux | FG Trupp d 597 | 15.11.41 |
| Mil.Verw.i.Fr.,Mil.Verw.Bez.Bordeaux | FG Trupp 651 | 15.11.41 |
| Mil.Verw.i.Fr.,Mil.Verw.Bez.Bordeaux | FG Trupp c (tmot) 657 | 15.11.41 |
| Mil.Verw.i.Fr.,Mil.Verw.Bez.Bordeaux | FG Trupp 659 der K.K. 659 | 15.11.41 |
| Mil.Verw.i.Fr.,Mil.Verw.Bez.Bordeaux | FG Trupp c (mot) 677 | 15.11.41 |
| Mil.Verw.i.Fr.,Mil.Verw.Bez.Bordeaux | FG Trupp 730 | 15.11.41 |
| Mil.Verw.i.Fr.,Mil.Verw.Bez.Bordeaux | FG Trupp 732 der K.K. 732 | 15.11.41 |
| Mil.Verw.i.Fr.,Mil.Verw.Bez.Bordeaux | FG Trupp 734 | 15.11.41 |
| Mil.Verw.i.Fr.,Mil.Verw.Bez.Bordeaux | FG Trupp 736 | 15.11.41 |
| Mil.Verw.i.Fr.,Mil.Verw.Bez.Bordeaux | FG Trupp d 739 | 15.11.41 |
| Mil.Verw.i.Fr.,Mil.Verw.Bez.Bordeaux | FG Trupp 764 | 15.11.41 |
| Mil.Verw.i.Fr.,Mil.Verw.Bez.Bordeaux | FG Trupp 777 | 15.11.41 |
| Mil.Verw.i.Fr.,Mil.Verw.Bez.Bordeaux | FG Trupp 779 | 15.11.41 |
| Mil.Verw.i.Fr.,Mil.Verw.Bez.Bordeaux | FG Trupp 860 | 15.11.41 |
| Mil.Verw.i.Fr.,Mil.Verw.Bez.Bordeaux | FG Trupp 539 | 27.11.42 |
| Mil.Verw.i.Fr.,Mil.Verw.Bez.C | F.K. 568/FG | 1.7.40 |
| Mil.Verw.i.Fr.,Mil.Verw.Bez.C | O.K. I/622 FG | 1.7.40 |
| Mil.Verw.i.Fr.,Mil.Verw.Bez.C | F.K. 560 FG | 2.7.40 |
| Mil.Verw.i.Fr.,Mil.Verw.Bez.C | F.K. 516 FG | 2.7.40 |
| Mil.Verw.i.Fr.,Mil.Verw.Bez.C | O.K. I/728 FG | 2.7.40 |
| Mil.Verw.i.Fr.,Mil.Verw.Bez.C | F.K. 590(V)FG | 5.7.40 |
| Mil.Verw.i.Fr.,Mil.Verw.Bez.C | O.K.II/739 FG Gruppe | 9.7.40 |
| Mil.Verw.i.Fr.,Mil.Verw.Bez.C | O.K.II/597 FG | 11.7.40 |
| Mil.Verw.i.Fr.,Mil.Verw.Bez.C | K.K. I/767 FG | 14.7.40 |
| Mil.Verw.i.Fr.,Mil.Verw.Bez.C | O.K.II/658/FG | 15.7.40 |
| Mil.Verw.i.Fr.,Mil.Verw.Bez.C | O.K.II/660/FG | 18.7.40 |
| Mil.Verw.i.Fr.,Mil.Verw.Bez.C | O.K. I/552 FG | 20.7.40 |
| Mil.Verw.i.Fr.,Mil.Verw.Bez.C | O.K.II/661/FG | 21.7.40 |
| Mil.Verw.i.Fr.,Mil.Verw.Bez.C | O.K.IV/760 FG | 23.7.40 |
| Mil.Verw.i.Fr.,Mil.Verw.Bez.C | O.K. I/594 FG | 24.7.40 |
| Mil.Verw.i.Fr.,Mil.Verw.Bez.C | O.K.II/558 FG | 25.7.40 |
| Mil.Verw.i.Fr.,Mil.Verw.Bez.C | O.K. I/629 FG | 26.7.40 |
| Mil.Verw.i.Fr.,Mil.Verw.Bez.C | O.K.II/596 FG | 30.7.40 |
| Mil.Verw.i.Fr.,Mil.Verw.Bez.C | O.K. I/627 FG | 30.7.40 |
| Mil.Verw.i.Fr.,Mil.Verw.Bez.C | O.K.II/656/FG | 30.7.40 |
| Mil.Verw.i.Fr.,Mil.Verw.Bez.C | O.K. I/726 FG | 30.7.40 |
| Mil.Verw.i.Fr.,Mil.Verw.Bez.C | O.K. I/727 FG | 30.7.40 |

| | | |
|---|---|---|
| Mil.Verw.i.Fr.,Mil.Verw.Bez.C | O.K.II/737 FG | 30.7.40 |
| Mil.Verw.i.Fr.,Mil.Verw.Bez.C | O.K.II/892 FG | 30.7.40 |
| Mil.Verw.i.Fr.,Mil.Verw.Bez.C | O.K. I/795 FG | 18.8.40 |
| Mil.Verw.i.Fr.,Mil.Verw.Bez.C | F.K. 590/FG | 10.9.40 |
| Mil.Verw.i.Fr.,Mil.Verw.Bez.C | K.K. 594/FG | 10.9.40 |
| Mil.Verw.i.Fr.,Mil.Verw.Bez.C | K.K. 596/FG | 10.9.40 |
| Mil.Verw.i.Fr.,Mil.Verw.Bez.C | K.K. 552/FG | 10.9.40 |
| Mil.Verw.i.Fr.,Mil.Verw.Bez.C | K.K. 558/FG | 10.9.40 |
| Mil.Verw.i.Fr.,Mil.Verw.Bez.C | O.K.II/620 FG | 10.9.40 |
| Mil.Verw.i.Fr.,Mil.Verw.Bez.C | K.K. 620/FG | 10.9.40 |
| Mil.Verw.i.Fr.,Mil.Verw.Bez.C | K.K. 622/FG | 10.9.40 |
| Mil.Verw.i.Fr.,Mil.Verw.Bez.C | K.K. 627/FG | 10.9.40 |
| Mil.Verw.i.Fr.,Mil.Verw.Bez.C | K.K. 629/FG | 10.9.40 |
| Mil.Verw.i.Fr.,Mil.Verw.Bez.C | K.K. 656/FG | 10.9.40 |
| Mil.Verw.i.Fr.,Mil.Verw.Bez.C | K.K. I/660/FG | 10.9.40 |
| Mil.Verw.i.Fr.,Mil.Verw.Bez.C | K.K. 661/FG | 10.9.40 |
| Mil.Verw.i.Fr.,Mil.Verw.Bez.C | K.K. 726/FG | 10.9.40 |
| Mil.Verw.i.Fr.,Mil.Verw.Bez.C | K.K. 727/FG | 10.9.40 |
| Mil.Verw.i.Fr.,Mil.Verw.Bez.C | K.K. I/728 FG | 10.9.40 |
| Mil.Verw.i.Fr.,Mil.Verw.Bez.C | K.K. 737 FG | 10.9.40 |
| Mil.Verw.i.Fr.,Mil.Verw.Bez.C | K.K. 760 FG | 10.9.40 |
| Mil.Verw.i.Fr.,Mil.Verw.Bez.C | F.K. 776 FG | 10.9.40 |
| Mil.Verw.i.Fr.,Mil.Verw.Bez.C | K.K. I/795 FG | 10.9.40 |
| Mil.Verw.i.Fr.,Mil.Verw.Bez.C (Dijon) | K.K. I/892 FG Trupp | 10.9.40 |
| Mil.Verw.i.Fr.,Mil.Verw.Bez.C | O.K.II/706/FG | 13.9.40 |
| Mil.Verw.i.Fr.,Mil.Verw.Bez.C | K.K. 893 FG | 1.10.40 |
| Mil.Verw.i.Fr.,Mil.Verw.Bez.C | FG Trupp 208 | 21.10.40 |
| Mil.Verw.i.Fr.,Mil.Verw.Bez.C | F.K. 590(F)/FG | 31.10.40 |
| Mil.Verw.i.Fr.,Mil.Verw.Bez.C | FG Trupp a (mot) 215 | 5.11.40 |
| Mil.Verw.i.Fr.,Mil.Verw.Bez.C | FG Trupp a (mot) 225 | 5.11.40 |
| Mil.Verw.i.Fr.,Mil.Verw.Bez.C | F.K. 516/FG Trupp a (mot) | 1.8.41 |
| Mil.Verw.i.Fr.,Mil.Verw.Bez.C | FG Trupp 727 | 17.8.41 |
| Mil.Verw.i.Fr.,Mil.Verw.Bez.C | FG Trupp a (mot) 590 | 15.11.41 |
| Mil.Verw.i.Fr.,Mil.Verw.Bez.C | FG Trupp 594 | 15.11.41 |
| Mil.Verw.i.Fr.,Mil.Verw.Bez.C | FG Trupp 596 | 15.11.41 |
| Mil.Verw.i.Fr.,Mil.Verw.Bez.C | FG Trupp a (mot) 550 | 15.11.41 |
| Mil.Verw.i.Fr.,Mil.Verw.Bez.C | FG Trupp 552 | 15.11.41 |
| Mil.Verw.i.Fr.,Mil.Verw.Bez.C | FG Trupp 558 | 15.11.41 |
| Mil.Verw.i.Fr.,Mil.Verw.Bez.C | FG Trupp 560 | 15.11.41 |
| Mil.Verw.i.Fr.,Mil.Verw.Bez.C | FG Trupp a (mot) 516 | 15.11.41 |
| Mil.Verw.i.Fr.,Mil.Verw.Bez.C | FG Trupp 622 | 15.11.41 |
| Mil.Verw.i.Fr.,Mil.Verw.Bez.C | FG Trupp 627 | 15.11.41 |
| Mil.Verw.i.Fr.,Mil.Verw.Bez.C | FG Trupp 629 | 15.11.41 |
| Mil.Verw.i.Fr.,Mil.Verw.Bez.C | FG Trupp 656 | 15.11.41 |
| Mil.Verw.i.Fr.,Mil.Verw.Bez.C | FG Trupp 658 | 15.11.41 |
| Mil.Verw.i.Fr.,Mil.Verw.Bez.C | FG Trupp 660 | 15.11.41 |
| Mil.Verw.i.Fr.,Mil.Verw.Bez.C | FG Trupp 661 | 15.11.41 |
| Mil.Verw.i.Fr.,Mil.Verw.Bez.C | FG Trupp 706 | 15.11.41 |
| Mil.Verw.i.Fr.,Mil.Verw.Bez.C | FG Trupp 726 | 15.11.41 |
| Mil.Verw.i.Fr.,Mil.Verw.Bez.C | FG Trupp 728 | 15.11.41 |
| Mil.Verw.i.Fr.,Mil.Verw.Bez.C | FG Trupp 737 | 15.11.41 |
| Mil.Verw.i.Fr.,Mil.Verw.Bez.C | K.K. 744/FG Trupp 744 | 15.11.41 |
| Mil.Verw.i.Fr.Mil.Verw.Bez. C | FG Trupp 760 | 15.11.41 |
| Mil.Verw.i.Fr.,Mil.Verw.Bez.C | FG Trupp 767 | 15.11.41 |

| Mil.Verw.i.Fr.,Mil.Verw.Bez.C | FG Trupp d 769 | 15.11.41 |
|---|---|---|
| Mil.Verw.i.Fr.,Mil.Verw.Bez.C | FG Trupp 795 | 15.11.41 |
| Mil.Verw.i.Fr.,Mil.Verw.Bez.C | FG Trupp 890 | 15.11.41 |
| Mil.Verw.i.Fr.,Mil.Verw.Bez.C (Dijon) | FG Trupp 892 | 15.11.41 |
| Mil.Verw.i.Fr.,Mil.Verw.Bez.C | FG Trupp 893 | 15.11.41 |
| Mil.Verw.i.Fr.,Mil.Verw.Bez.C | FG Trupp 901 | 9.1.42 |
| Mil.Verw.i.Fr.,Mil.Verw.Bez.C | FG Trupp 908 | 30.3.42 |
| Mil.Verw.i.Fr.,Mil.Verw.Bez.C | FG Trupp 925 | 7.4.42 |
| Mil.Verw.i.Fr.,Mil.Verw.Bez.C | FG Gruppe 998 | 14.12.42 |
| Mil.Verw.i.Fr.,Mil.Verw.Bez.C | FG Trupp 620 | 15.11.44 |

**Oberbefehlshaber (Commander)**

| Ob.Sued. | FG Trupp (mot) 498 | 30.6.43 |
|---|---|---|
| Ob.Sued. | FG Trupp a (mot) 476 | 5.7.43 |
| Ob.Suedost | FG Trupp c (tmot) 858 | 17.3.43 |
| Ob.Suedost | FG Trupp d 662 | 7.9.43 |
| Ob.Suedost | FG Trupp d 663 | 7.9.43 |
| Ob.Suedost | FG Trupp d 666 | 7.9.43 |
| Ob.Suedost | FG Trupp d 670 | 7.9.43 |
| Ob.Suedost | FG Trupp d 671 | 7.9.43 |
| Ob.Suedost | FG Trupp d 672 | 7.9.43 |
| Ob.Suedost | FG Trupp d 674 | 7.9.43 |
| Ob.Suedost | FG Trupp d (tmot) 1152 | 14.1.45 |
| Ob.Suedost (Obkdo.H.Gr.E) | Stab, FG Abt (mot) 501 | 1.1.43 |
| Ob.Suedost (Obkdo.H.Gr.E) | 1.Kp. FG Abt (mot) 501 | 1.1.43 |
| Ob.Suedwest | FG Trupp 652 | 11.12.43 |
| Ob.Suedwest | FG Trupp d 653 | 11.12.43 |
| Ob.Suedwest | FG Trupp c (tmot) 909 | 14.1.45 |
| Ob.Suedwest | FG Trupp 910 | 14.1.45 |
| Ob.Suedwest | FG Trupp d (tmot) 911 | 14.1.45 |
| Ob.Suedwest | FG Trupp 912 | 14.1.45 |
| Ob.West | FG Trupp c (tmot) 264 | 4.8.43 |
| Ob.West (13. Fliegerkorps) | FG Trupp a (mot) 675 | 17.11.43 |

**Oberkommando, Heeres Gruppe (High Command, Group of Armies)**

| Obkdo.H.Gr.A | FG Trupp d (tmot) 1046 | 14.1.45 |
|---|---|---|
| Obkdo.H.Gr.A | FG Trupp d (tmot) 1047 | 14.1.45 |
| Obkdo.H.Gr.B | FG Gruppe 1009 | 16.9.43 |
| Obkdo.H.Gr.B | FG Gruppe 1010 | 16.9.43 |
| Obkdo.H.Gr.B | FG Gruppe 1011 | 16.9.43 |
| Obkdo.H.Gr.B | FG Gruppe 1012 | 16.9.43 |
| Obkdo.H.Gr.B | FG Gruppe 1013 | 16.9.43 |

**Oberfeldkommandantur (Area Headquarters)**

| Oberfeldkommandantur 226 | FG Trupp 899 b | 6.9.44 |
|---|---|---|
| Oberfeldkommandantur 379 | FG Trupp c (tmot) 917 | 24.6.42 |
| Oberfeldkommandantur 379 | Stab, 1.-3.Kp., FG Abt 551 | 8.7.43 |
| Oberfeldkommandantur 520 | FG Trupp a (mot) 843 | ? |
| Oberfeldkommandantur 520 | FG Trupp d 839 | ? |
| Oberfeldkommandantur 520 | FG Trupp d 844 | ? |
| Oberfeldkommandantur 520 | FG Trupp d 845 | ? |
| Oberfeldkommandantur 520 | FG Trupp d 846 | ? |
| Oberfeldkommandantur 520 | FG Trupp d 851 | ? |
| Oberfeldkommandantur 520 | FG Trupp d 856 | ? |
| Oberfeldkommandantur 520 | O.K.II/703 FG Trupp | 2.6.40 |
| Oberfeldkommandantur 520 | FG Trupp a 183 | 25.1.41 |
| Oberfeldkommandantur 520 | O.K.II/703 FG Trupp | 28.2.41 |

| | | |
|---|---|---|
| Oberfeldkommandantur 520 | FG Trupp 838 | 27.10.41 |
| Oberfeldkommandantur 520 | G Trupp a (mot) 838 | 27.10.41 |
| Oberfeldkommandantur 570 | FG Trupp 840 | ? |
| Oberfeldkommandantur 570 | FG Trupp 848 | ? |
| Oberfeldkommandantur 570 | FG Trupp 849 | ? |
| Oberfeldkommandantur 570 | FG Trupp a (mot) 842 | ? |
| Oberfeldkommandantur 570 | FG Trupp a (mot) 854 | ? |
| Oberfeldkommandantur 570 | FG Trupp d 841 | ? |
| Oberfeldkommandantur 570 | FG Trupp d 847 | ? |
| Oberfeldkommandantur 570 | FG Trupp d 850 | ? |
| Oberfeldkommandantur 570 | FG Trupp d 852 | ? |
| Oberfeldkommandantur 570 | FG Trupp d 855 | ? |
| Oberfeldkommandantur 570 | O.K.II/703 FG Trupp | 14.4.40 |
| Oberfeldkommandantur 589 | FG Trupp a (mot) 807 | ? |
| Oberfeldkommandantur 589 | FG Trupp a (mot) 837 | ? |
| Oberfeldkommandantur 589 | FG Trupp d 802 | ? |
| Oberfeldkommandantur 589 | FG Trupp d 803 | ? |
| Oberfeldkommandantur 589 | FG Trupp d 804 | ? |
| Oberfeldkommandantur 589 | FG Trupp d 808 | ? |
| Oberfeldkommandantur 589 | FG Trupp d 812 | ? |
| Oberfeldkommandantur 591 | O.K.II/FG | 26.8.39 |
| Oberfeldkommandantur 591 | O.K. 626/FG Gruppe | 12.2.40 |
| Oberfeldkommandantur 592 | O.K. I/645 FG | 27.1.40 |
| Oberfeldkommandantur 592 | F.K. FG Gruppe | 7.3.40 |
| Oberfeldkommandantur 592 | F.K. 602/FG | 14.4.40 |
| Oberfeldkommandantur 592 | F.K. 684/FG | 18.4.40 |
| Oberfeldkommandantur 592 | FG Trupp d der O.K. I(V)/612 | 10.5.40 |
| Oberfeldkommandantur 670 | FG Trupp a (mot) 813 | ? |
| Oberfeldkommandantur 670 | FG Trupp a (mot) 815 | ? |
| Oberfeldkommandantur 670 | FG Trupp a (mot) 823 | ? |
| Oberfeldkommandantur 670 | FG Trupp a 806 | ? |
| Oberfeldkommandantur 670 | FG Trupp a 809 | ? |
| Oberfeldkommandantur 670 | FG Trupp a 814 | ? |
| Oberfeldkommandantur 670 | FG Trupp a 816 | ? |
| Oberfeldkommandantur 670 | FG Trupp a 818 | ? |
| Oberfeldkommandantur 670 | FG Trupp a 822 | ? |
| Oberfeldkommandantur 670 | FG Trupp a 824 | ? |
| Oberfeldkommandantur 670 | FG Trupp c (tmot) 833 | ? |
| Oberfeldkommandantur 670 | O.K.II/703 FG Trupp | 1.3.41 |
| Oberfeldkommandantur 672 | FG Trupp a (mot) 810 | ? |
| Oberfeldkommandantur 672 | FG Trupp a (mot) 820 | ? |
| Oberfeldkommandantur 672 | FG Trupp c (mot) 811 | ? |
| Oberfeldkommandantur 672 | FG Trupp c (mot) 831 | ? |
| Oberfeldkommandantur 672 | FG Trupp c (mot) 836 | ? |
| Oberfeldkommandantur 672 | FG Trupp d 817 | ? |
| Oberfeldkommandantur 672 | FG Trupp d 829 | ? |
| Oberfeldkommandantur 672 | FG Trupp d 830 | ? |
| Oberfeldkommandantur 672 | FG Trupp a (mot) 182 | 21.11.40 |
| Oberfeldkommandantur 672 | FG Trupp (mot) 193 | 23.11.40 |
| Oberfeldkommandantur 680 | F.K. 723/FG | 29.6.40 |
| Oberfeldkommandantur Krakau | FG Trupp b (mot) 899 | 1.1.42 |
| Oberfeldkommandantur Lemberg | FG Trupp d 508 | 18.8.43 |
| Oberfeldkommandantur Lublin | FG Trupp d (tmot) 1141 | 15.5.44 |
| Oberfeldkommandantur Warschau | FG Kp. 914 | 16.7.42 |

| | | |
|---|---|---|
| Oberfeldkommandantur Warschau | FG Trupp b (mot) 897 | 16.7.42 |
| Oberfeldkommandantur Warschau | FG Trupp c (tmot) 914 | 16.7.42 |
| Oberfeldkommandantur Warschau | FG Trupp d 507 | 18.8.43 |

**Ortskommandantur (Station Headquarters)**

| | | |
|---|---|---|
| Ortskommandantur 510 | FG Trupp d 841 | ? |
| Ortskommandantur 511 (Ostpr.) | FG Trupp 511 | 16.8.39 |
| Ortskommandantur 543 | O.K. I/543 FG Trupp | 26.8.39 |
| Ortskommandantur 584 | FG Trupp 584 | 26.8.39 |
| Ortskommandantur 592 | O.K.II/592 FG | 9.17.40 |
| Ortskommandantur 613 | FG Trupp d 845 | ? |
| Ortskommandantur 614 | FG Trupp d 839 | ? |
| Ortskommandantur 616 | FG Trupp d 851 | ? |
| Ortskommandantur 620 | O.K.II/620 FG | 26.8.39 |
| Ortskommandantur 626 | O.K. 626/FG Gruppe | 17.10.39 |
| Ortskommandantur 630 | FG Trupp 840 | ? |
| Ortskommandantur 632 | FG Trupp d 850 | ? |
| Ortskommandantur 635 | FG Trupp d 832 | ? |
| Ortskommandantur 636 | FG Trupp d 812 | ? |
| Ortskommandantur 639 | FG Trupp d 805 | ? |
| Ortskommandantur 642 | FG Trupp a 806 | ? |
| Ortskommandantur 643 | FG Trupp d 827 | ? |
| Ortskommandantur 649 | O.K. I/649 FG | 27.8.39 |
| Ortskommandantur 652 | FG Trupp d 852 | ? |
| Ortskommandantur 654 | FG Trupp 848 | ? |
| Ortskommandantur 663 | FG Trupp d 855 | ? |
| Ortskommandantur 687 | FG Trupp d 804 | ? |
| Ortskommandantur 688 | FG Trupp d 844 | ? |
| Ortskommandantur 689 | FG Trupp d 817 | ? |
| Ortskommandantur 690 | FG Trupp d 847 | ? |
| Ortskommandantur 691 | FG Trupp d 808 | ? |
| Ortskommandantur 691 | FG Trupp d 39 | 13.9.41 |
| Ortskommandantur 691 | FG Trupp 808 | 27.10.41 |
| Ortskommandantur 692 | FG Trupp a 818 | ? |
| Ortskommandantur 693 | FG Trupp d 819 | ? |
| Ortskommandantur 694 | FG Trupp d 829 | ? |
| Ortskommandantur 699 | FG Trupp d 801 | ? |
| Ortskommandantur 699 | O.K. I/699 FG Gruppe | 5.1.40 |
| Ortskommandantur 699 | O.K. I/699 FG Trupp d | 13.9.41 |
| Ortskommandantur 699 | O.K. I/699 FG Trupp d 801 | 27.10.41 |
| Ortskommandantur 701 | FG Trupp d 802 | ? |
| Ortskommandantur 702 | FG Trupp d 830 | ? |
| Ortskommandantur 703 | FG Trupp a 814 | ? |
| Ortskommandantur 703 | O.K.II/703 FG Trupp | 6.1.40 |
| Ortskommandantur 705 | FG Trupp d 846 | ? |
| Ortskommandantur 707 | FG Trupp a 822 | ? |
| Ortskommandantur 708 | FG Trupp 849 | ? |
| Ortskommandantur 713 | FG Trupp d 834 | ? |
| Ortskommandantur 714 | FG Trupp a 824 | ? |
| Ortskommandantur 715 | FG Trupp a 809 | ? |
| Ortskommandantur 718 | FG Trupp c (tmot) 718 | 6.2.43 |
| Ortskommandantur 726 | O.K. I/726 FG | 20.5.40 |
| Ortskommandantur 727 | O.K. I/727 FG | 20.5.40 |
| Ortskommandantur 728 | O.K. I/728 FG | 20.5.40 |
| Ortskommandantur 729 | O.K. I/729 FG | 18.5.40 |

| | | |
|---|---|---|
| Ortskommandantur 730 | O.K. I/730 FG | 22.5.40 |
| Ortskommandantur 731 | O.K. I/731 FG | 21.5.40 |
| Ortskommandantur 732 | O.K. I/732 FG Gruppe | 20.5.40 |
| Ortskommandantur 733 | O.K. I/733 FG | 20.5.40 |
| Ortskommandantur 734 | O.K. I/734 FG | 20.5.40 |
| Ortskommandantur 735 | O.K. I/735 FG | 20.5.40 |
| Ortskommandantur 736 | O.K.II/736 FG | 20.5.40 |
| Ortskommandantur 737 | O.K.II/737 FG | 20.5.40 |
| Ortskommandantur 738 | O.K.II/738 FG | 20.5.40 |
| Ortskommandantur 738 | FG Trupp d 738 | 15.9.40 |
| Ortskommandantur 739 | O.K.II/739 FG Gruppe | 18.5.40 |
| Ortskommandantur 740 | FG Trupp der O.K. 740 | 27.5.40 |
| Ortskommandantur 741 | O.K.II/741 FG | 20.5.40 |
| Ortskommandantur 742 | O.K.II/742 FG | 20.5.40 |
| Ortskommandantur 759 | O.K. I (V) 759 FG | 10.6.40 |
| Ortskommandantur 760 | O.K.IV/760 FG | 11.6.40 |
| Ortskommandantur 764 | O.K. I/764 FG | 15.6.40 |
| Ortskommandantur 768 | O.K. I(V) 768 FG | 12.6.40 |
| Ortskommandantur 771 | FG Trupp d 825 | ? |
| Ortskommandantur 772 | FG Trupp d 828 | ? |
| Ortskommandantur 776 | O.K. I/776 FG Gruppe | 29.5.40 |
| Ortskommandantur 777 | O.K. I/777 FG | 20.5.40 |
| Ortskommandantur 779 | O.K. I/779 FG | 3.6.40 |
| Ortskommandantur 780 | O.K.II/780 FG Trupp | 3.6.40 |
| Ortskommandantur 781 | O.K.II/781 FG | 3.6.40 |
| Ortskommandantur 786 | O.K. I(V) 786 FG | 10.9.40 |
| Ortskommandantur 789 | O.K. I(V) 789 FG | 2.8.40 |
| Ortskommandantur 794 | O.K. I/794 FG Gruppe | 1.8.40 |
| Ortskommandantur 795 | O.K. I/795 FG | 1.8.40 |
| Ortskommandantur 796 | O.K. I(V) 796 FG | 1.8.40 |
| Ortskommandantur 797 | O.K. 797 FG | 1.8.40 |
| Ortskommandantur 802 | O.K. I (V)/802 FG Gruppe | 7.8.40 |
| Ortskommandantur 803 | O.K. I (V)/803 FG | 1.8.40 |
| Ortskommandantur 806 | O.K. I(V) 806 FG Trupp | 2.8.40 |
| Ortskommandantur 807 | O.K.II(V)/807 FG Trupp | 6.8.40 |
| Ortskommandantur 825 | O.K. I(V) 825/FG | 24.7.42 |
| Ortskommandantur 832 | O.K. I/832 FG Gruppe | 6.8.40 |
| Ortskommandantur 833 | O.K. I (V)/833 FG Gruppe | 7.8.40 |
| Ortskommandantur 834 | O.K. I/834 FG Gruppe | 8.8.40 |
| Ortskommandantur 838 | O.K. I/838 FG Gruppe | 7.8.40 |
| Ortskommandantur 855 | O.K. I(V) 855/FG | 24.7.42 |
| Ortskommandantur 856 | O.K. I(V) 856/FG | 24.7.42 |
| Ortskommandantur 857 | O.K. I/857 FG Gruppe | 8.8.40 |
| Ortskommandantur 861 | O.K. I/861 FG Gruppe | 7.8.40 |
| Ortskommandantur 866 | O.K. I(V) 866/FG | 24.7.42 |
| Ortskommandantur 867 | O.K. I/867 FG Gruppe | 10.8.40 |
| Ortskommandantur 888 | O.K. 888/FG | 11.9.40 |
| Ortskommandantur 891 | FG Trupp d 960 | 6.5.43 |
| Ortskommandantur 892 (Dresden) | O.K.II/892 FG | 26.8.39 |
| Ortskommandantur 895 | O.K. 895 FG Trupp d | 9.9.40 |
| Ortskommandantur 913 | FG Trupp d 826 | ? |
| Ortskommandantur 914 | FG Trupp a 816 | ? |
| Ortskommandantur 940 | FG Trupp d 803 | ? |
| Ortskommandantur 942 | FG Trupp d 856 | ? |

| | | |
|---|---|---|
| Ortskommandantur Smolensk | FG Trupp d der O.K. Smolensk | 24.7.42 |

**Rheinbrueckenkommandantur (Rhine Bridge Headquarters)**

| | | |
|---|---|---|
| Rheinbruckenkdtr. 33 (Hoeh.Kdo.33) | O.K. I/622 | 11.6.40 |

**Wehrkreis (Military Sevice Command)**

| | | |
|---|---|---|
| W.K. 6 | FG Trupp 843 | ? |
| W.K. 6 | FG Trupp 846 | ? |
| W.K. 6 | FG Trupp 856 | ? |
| W.K. 9 | FG Trupp 809 | 29.1.40 |
| W.K. 9 | O.K. I/884 FG | 12.9.40 |
| W.K. 13 | FG Trupp 766 | ? |
| W.K. 13 | FG Trupp 770 | ? |
| W.K. 13 | FG Trupp 788 | ? |
| W.K. 13 | FG Trupp 798 | ? |
| W.K. 13 | FG Trupp 885 | 19.10.44 |
| W.K. 20 | FG Kp. (mot) 757 | 24.10.42 |
| W.K. 21 | FG Trupp 1062 | 11.12.43 |
| W.K. 21 | FG Trupp 1063 | 11.12.43 |
| W.K. 21 | FG Trupp 1064 | 11.12.43 |
| W.K. 21 | FG Trupp d 1110 | 4.5.44 |
| W.K. 21 | FG Trupp d 1109 | 4.5.44 |
| W.K. 21 | FG Trupp c (mot) 1340 | 22.9.44 |

**Wehrkreis Boehmen-Maehren (Military Service Command Bohemia-Moravia)**

| | | |
|---|---|---|
| W.K. Boehmen-Maehren | FG Trupp 830 | ? |
| W.K. Boehmen-Maehren | FG Trupp a (mot) z.V. 1901 | 25.1.45 |
| W.K. Boehmen-Maehren | FG Trupp a (mot) z.V. 1902 | 25.1.45 |
| W.K. Boehmen-Maehren | FG Trupp a (mot) z.V. 1903 | 25.1.45 |
| W.K. Boehmen-Maehren | FG Trupp a (mot) z.V. 2901 | 25.1.45 |
| W.K. Boehmen-Maehren | FG Trupp a (mot) z.V. 2902 | 25.1.45 |
| W.K. Boehmen-Maehren | FG Trupp a (mot) z.V. 2903 | 25.1.45 |
| W.K. Boehmen-Maehren | FG Trupp a (mot) z.V. 3901 | 25.1.45 |
| W.K. Boehmen-Maehren | FG Trupp a (mot) z.V. 3902 | 25.1.45 |
| W.K. Boehmen-Maehren | FG Trupp a (mot) z.V. 3903 | 25.1.45 |

**Wehrkreis Generalgouvernement (Military Service Command Poland)**

| | | |
|---|---|---|
| W.K. Gen.Gouv. | FG Trupp c (tmot) 916 | 1.4.42 |
| W.K. Gen.Gouv. | FG Trupp b (mot) 934 | 21.1.43 |
| W.K. Gen.Gouv. | FG Trupp b (mot) 935 | 21.1.43 |
| W.K. Gen.Gouv. | FG Trupp d (mot) 936 | 21.1.43 |
| W.K. Gen.Gouv. | FG Trupp d (mot) 937 | 21.1.43 |
| W.K. Gen.Gouv. | FG Trupp d (mot) 938 | 21.1.43 |
| W.K. Gen.Gouv. | FG Trupp d (mot) 939 | 21.1.43 |
| W.K. Gen.Gouv. | FG Trupp d (mot) 940 | 21.1.43 |
| W.K. Gen.Gouv. | FG Trupp d (mot) 942 | 21.1.43 |
| W.K. Gen.Gouv. | FG Trupp d (mot) 943 | 21.1.43 |
| W.K. Gen.Gouv. | FG Trupp d (mot) 944 | 21.1.43 |
| W.K. Gen.Gouv. | FG Trupp d (mot) 945 | 21.1.43 |
| W.K. Gen.Gouv. | FG Trupp d (mot) 946 | 21.1.43 |
| W.K. Gen.Gouv. | FG Trupp d (mot) 947 | 21.1.43 |
| W.K. Gen.Gouv. | FG Trupp d (mot) 948 | 21.1.43 |
| W.K. Gen.Gouv. | FG Trupp d (mot) 949 | 21.1.43 |
| W.K. Gen.Gouv. | FG Trupp d (mot) 950 | 21.1.43 |
| W.K. Gen.Gouv. | FG Trupp d (mot) 951 | 21.1.43 |
| W.K. Gen.Gouv. | FG Trupp d (mot) 952 | 21.1.43 |
| W.K. Gen.Gouv. | FG Trupp 953 | 21.1.43 |
| W.K. Gen.Gouv. | FG Trupp 954 | 21.1.43 |

| | | |
|---|---|---|
| W.K. Gen.Gouv. | FG Trupp 955 | 21.1.43 |
| W.K. Gen.Gouv. | FG Trupp 956 | 21.1.43 |
| W.K. Gen.Gouv. | FG Trupp 957 | 21.1.43 |
| W.K. Gen.Gouv. | FG Trupp d (tmot) 1016 | 3.5.44 |

**Wehrkreiskommandant (Military Service Command, Commanding Officer)**

| | | |
|---|---|---|
| W.K.Kdt. 9 | O.K. I/695/FG Trupp | 7.1.40 |
| W.K.Kdt.21 | O.K. I/533 FG | 26.10.39 |

**Wehr Ersatz Kommando (Recruiting Command)**

| | | |
|---|---|---|
| Wehr Ersatz Kommando 1 | FG Staffel des alten WEK 1005 | 3.6.43 |
| Wehr Ersatz Kommando 1 | FG Staffel des neuen WEK 1001 | 3.6.43 |
| Wehr Ersatz Kommando 2 | FG Staffel des alten WEK 1002 | 3.6.43 |
| Wehr Ersatz Kommando 3 | FG Staffel des neuen WEK 1003 | 3.6.43 |
| Wehr Ersatz Kommando 4 | FG Staffel des neuen WEK 1004 | 3.6.43 |
| Wehr Ersatz Kommando 7 | FG Staffel des alten WEK 1006 | 3.6.43 |

**Wehrmacht Befehlshaber (Armed Forces Commander)**

| | | |
|---|---|---|
| Wehrm. Befh. Daenemark | FG Trupp d 881 | 27.4.43 |
| Wehrm. Befh. Sudost | FG Trupp 920 | 9.8.42 |
| Wehrm. Befh. Sudost | FG Trupp 922 | 9.8.42 |
| Wehrm. Befh. Sudost | FG Trupp 919 | 12.8.42 |
| Wehrm. Befh. Sudost | FG Trupp 921 | 12.8.42 |
| Wehrm. Befh. Sudost (A.O.K. 12) | 2.Kp. FG Abt (mot) 501 | 27.1.42 |
| Wehrm. Befh. Sudost (A.O.K. 12) | Stab, FG Abt (mot) 501 | 28.1.42 |
| Wehrm. Befh. Sudost (A.O.K. 12) | 1.Kp. FG Abt (mot) 501 | 28.7.42 |

**Wehrmacht Kommandantur (Armed Forces Headquarters)**

| | | |
|---|---|---|
| Wehrm.Kdtr.Amsterdam | FG Trupp d (tmot) 1147 | 9.8.44 |
| Wehrm.Kdtr.Minsk | FG Trupp d (tmot) 1148 | 9.8.44 |
| Wehrm.Kdtr.Rotterdam | FG Trupp d (tmot) 1144 | 9.8.44 |

**Wehrmacht Ortskommandantur (Armed Forces Station Headquarters)**

| | | |
|---|---|---|
| Wehrm.Ortskdtr.Gross Kopenhagen | FG Trupp d (tmot) der Wehrm.O.K.G.K. | 13.4.44 |
| Wehrm.Ortskdtr.Gross Kopenhagen | FG Trupp d (tmot) 998 | 18.4.44 |
| Wehrm.Ortskdtr.Riga | FG Trupp d (tmot) 1149 | 9.8.44 |

## KORPS

**Armee Korps (Army Corps)**

| | | |
|---|---|---|
| 1. A.K. | FG Trupp 421 | 1.8.39 |
| 3. A.K. | FG Trupp a (mot) 403 | 26.8.39 |
| 4. A.K. | FG Abt (mot) 683 | 7.10.39 |
| 4. A.K. | F.K. 723/FG | 20.5.40 |
| 6. A.K. | FG Trupp a (mot) 406 | 25.8.39 |
| 7. A.K. | FG Trupp 407 | ? |
| 10. A.K. | FG Trupp a (mot) 410 | 26.8.39 |
| 12. A.K. | FG Trupp 412 | 27.8.39 |
| 14. A.K. | FG Trupp b (mot) 414 | 18.8.39 |
| 15. (Gebirgs) A.K. | FG Trupp b 415 | 12.8.43 |
| 15. A.K. | FG Trupp b 415 | 19.8.39 |
| 16. A.K. | FG Trupp b (mot) 473 | 19.8.39 |
| 16. A.K. | O.K. I/542 FG | 1.1.40 |
| 16. A.K. | 3.Kp. FG Abt (mot) 501 | 8.6.40 |
| 17. A.K. | Stab, FG Abt (mot) 521 | 3.8.39 |
| 17. A.K. | 1.Kp. FG Abt (mot) 521 | 3.8.39 |
| 17. A.K. | 2.Kp. FG Abt (mot) 521 | 3.8.39 |
| 17. A.K. | FG Trupp a (mot) 417 | 6.8.39 |
| 17. A.K. (Wien) | 3.Kp. FG Abt (mot) 521 | 4.8.39 |
| 18. (Gebirgs) A.K. | FG Trupp 449 | 15.12.40 |

| | | |
|---|---|---|
| 18. (Gebirgs) A.K. | FG Trupp 418 | 21.12.43 |
| 18. A.K. | FG Trupp a (mot) 418 | 10.8.39 |
| 19. (Gebirgs) A.K. | FG Trupp 419 | 23.12.43 |
| 19. A.K. | FG Trupp b (mot) 419 | 18.8.39 |
| 21. (Gebirgs) A.K. | FG Trupp 421 | 12.8.43 |
| 22. (Gebirgs) A.K. | FG Trupp b (mot) 422 | 12.8.43 |
| 22. A.K. | FG Abt (mot) 685 (mit 2,3 Kp) | 2.9.39 |
| 23. A.K. | FG Trupp a (mot) 308 | 25.8.39 |
| 23. A.K. | FG Trupp a (mot) 308 | 26.8.39 |
| 23. A.K. | FG Trupp a (mot) 423 | 1.4.41 |
| 24. A.K. | FG Trupp (mot) 311 | 26.8.39 |
| 24. A.K. (262. I.D.) | O.K.II/592 FG | 1.11.39 |
| 24. A.K. (Feldkdtr.591) | O.K.II/592 FG | 2.6.40 |
| 24. Panzer Kps. | FG Trupp 424 | 27.11.44 |
| 25. A.K. | FG Trupp 555 | 7.7.40 |
| 25. A.K. | FG Trupp 307 | 1.11.40 |
| 27. A.K. | FG Trupp a (mot) 236 | 24.12.40 |
| 27. A.K. | FG Trupp a 427 | 28.7.44 |
| 30. A.K. | O.K. I/594 FG | 18.6.40 |
| 35. A.K. | FG Trupp 435 | 20.7.44 |
| 38. A.K. | FG Trupp 438 | 27.1.40 |
| 39. A.K. | FG Trupp a (mot) 439 | 28.1.40 |
| 39. A.K. | FG Trupp b (mot) 439 | 1.3.40 |
| 42. A.K. | FG Trupp a (mot) 442 | 26.1.40 |
| 42. A.K. | FG Trupp 360 | 21.5.44 |
| 44. A.K. | FG Trupp (mot) 444 | 15.4.40 |
| 49. (Gebirgs) A.K. | FG Trupp a (mot) 418 | 30.10.40 |
| 49. (Gebirgs) A.K. | FG Trupp 449 | 18.3.44 |
| 51. A.K. | FG Trupp a (mot) 451 | 30.1.41 |
| 53. A.K. | FG Trupp 453 | ? |
| 66. A.K. | FG Trupp 612 | 15.10.44 |
| 67. A.K. | FG Trupp 467 | 18.3.44 |
| 71. A.K. | FG Trupp z.b.V. 71 | 10.42 |
| 71. A.K. | FG Trupp (mot) 230 | 15.2.43 |
| 71. A.K. | FG Trupp (mot) 930 | 5.43 |
| 88. A.K. | FG Trupp c (tmot) 617 | 10.9.42 |
| Gebirgs Korp Norwegen | FG Trupp (mot) 463 | 12.9.40 |
| Korps | FG Trupp 430 | ? |
| Korps | FG Trupp a (mot) 441 | 1.2.40 |
| Korps | FG Trupp (mot) 433 | 5.4.40 |
| Korps | FG Trupp b (mot) 441 | 3.8.44 |
| Korps-Abt. | FG Trupp 241 | 28.3.44 |
| Korps-Abt.B | FG Trupp 112 | 28.3.44 |
| Korps-Abt.C | FG Trupp a (mot) 219 | 28.3.44 |
| Korps-Abt.E | FG Trupp a (mot) 251 | 28.3.44 |
| Korps-Abt.H | FG Trupp a (mot) 256 | 13.7.44 |
| Korpskommando 12 | FG Trupp (mot) 317 | 7.12.39 |
| Panzerkorps.Feldherrnhalle | FG Trupp a (mot) 404 | 27.11.44 |
| Panzerkorps.Grossdeutschland | FG Trupp b (mot) 500 | 13.12.44 |
| **Fallschirmjaegerkorps (Paratrooper Corps)** | | |
| I. Fallschirmjaegerkorps | FG Trupp b (mot) 676 | 13.1.44 |
| II. Fallschirmjaegerkorps | FG Trupp b (mot) 675 | 10.5.44 |
| **Generalkommando (Corps Headquarters)** | | |
| Gen.Kdo. | FG Trupp c (mot) 282 | 7.1.43 |

| | | | |
|---|---|---|---|
| Gen.Kdo. | | FG Trupp c (mot) 282 | 12.1.43 |
| Gen.Kdo. 1. A.K. | | FG Gruppe der O.K. I(V) 505 | 26.8.39 |
| Gen.Kdo. 1. A.K. | | FG Trupp 401 | 28.2.44 |
| Gen.Kdo. 2. A.K. | | O.K.II/609 FG | 26.8.39 |
| Gen.Kdo. 2. A.K. | | O.K. I/607 FG | 27.8.39 |
| Gen.Kdo. 4. A.K. | | FG Gruppe der F.K. 541 | 15.8.39 |
| Gen.Kdo. 4. A.K. | | F.K. 602/FG | 26.11.39 |
| Gen.Kdo. 4. A.K. | | F.K. 540/FG | 20.5.40 |
| Gen.Kdo. 4. A.K. | | FG Trupp a (mot) 404 | 2.8.43 |
| Gen.Kdo. 4. Luftwaffe Feldkorps | | FG Trupp Gen.Kdo.4.Lw.F.Korps | 30.11.42 |
| Gen.Kdo. 4. Panzer Kps. | | FG Trupp a (mot) 404 | 8.10.44 |
| Gen.Kdo. 5. A.K. | | FG Trupp (mot) 405 | 26.8.39 |
| Gen.Kdo. 5. A.K. | | F.K. 550 FG | 26.8.39 |
| Gen.Kdo. 5. A.K. | | O.K. I/552 FG | 26.8.39 |
| Gen.Kdo. 5. A.K. | | F.K. 605/FG | 26.9.39 |
| Gen.Kdo. 5. A.K. | | O.K. I/621 FG | 17.10.39 |
| Gen.Kdo. 5. A.K. | | O.K.II/655/FG | 18.10.39 |
| Gen.Kdo. 5. A.K. | | O.K. I/622 | 19.10.39 |
| Gen.Kdo. 5. A.K. | | Stab, FG Abt 551 | 6.8.40 |
| Gen.Kdo. 5. A.K. | | FG Trupp c (tmot) 618 | 20.8.42 |
| Gen.Kdo. 5. A.K. | | FG Trupp a (mot) 405 (neu) | 26.1.45 |
| Gen.Kdo. 5. A.K. (Stuttgart) | | O.K. I/553 FG | 26.8.39 |
| Gen.Kdo. 6. A.K. | | F.K. 560 FG | 26.8.39 |
| Gen.Kdo. 6. A.K. | | O.K. I/564 FG | 26.8.39 |
| Gen.Kdo. 6. A.K. | | O.K. I/563 FG | 20.5.40 |
| Gen.Kdo. 7. A.K. | | FG Trupp der K.K. 657 | 26.10.40 |
| Gen.Kdo. 7. Panzer Kps. | | FG Trupp 407 | 18.12.44 |
| Gen.Kdo. 8. A.K. | | O.K. I/793 FG | 4.8.40 |
| Gen.Kdo. 8. A.K. | | F.K. 516/FG | 11.9.39 |
| Gen.Kdo. 8. A.K. | | O.K.II/706 FG | 10.10.39 |
| Gen.Kdo. 8. A.K. | | Stab, FG Abt 551 | 10.8.40 |
| Gen.Kdo. 8. A.K. | | FG Trupp a (mot) 408 | 2.8.43 |
| Gen.Kdo. 9. A.K. | | FG Trupp 409 | 25.8.39 |
| Gen.Kdo. 9. A.K. | | O.K.II/596 FG | 26.8.39 |
| Gen.Kdo. 9. A.K. | | O.K.II/597 FG | 26.8.39 |
| Gen.Kdo. 9. A.K. | | O.K. I/594 FG | 18.9.39 |
| Gen.Kdo. 9. A.K. | | O.K. I/629 FG | 16.10.39 |
| Gen.Kdo. 9. A.K. | | O.K. I/627 FG | 17.10.39 |
| Gen.Kdo. 9. A.K. | | O.K. I/645 FG | 29.10.39 |
| Gen.Kdo. 9. A.K. | | O.K.II/665/FG | 29.10.39 |
| Gen.Kdo. 9. A.K. | | FG Trupp 584 | 26.11.39 |
| Gen.Kdo. 9. A.K. (Kassel) | | O.K. I/695 (V) FG | 1.4.40 |
| Gen.Kdo.10. A.K. | | FG Trupp der K.K. 659 | 30.9.40 |
| Gen.Kdo.10. A.K. (Hamburg) | | O.K. I/651 FG | 28.10.39 |
| Gen.Kdo.11. A.K. | | O.K.II/660/FG | 15.10.39 |
| Gen.Kdo.11. A.K. | | FG Abt (mot) 685 (mit 1,2,3 Kp) | 27.10.39 |
| Gen.Kdo.11. A.K. | | F.K. 677/FG | 27.1.40 |
| Gen.Kdo.11. A.K. | | Stab, FG Abt (mot) 696 | 2.5.41 |
| Gen.Kdo.11. A.K. | | 1.Kp FG Abt (mot) 696 | 2.5.41 |
| Gen.Kdo.11. A.K. | | 2.Kp. FG Abt (mot) 696 | 2.5.41 |
| Gen.Kdo.11. A.K. | | 3.Kp. FG Abt (mot) 696 | 2.5.41 |
| Gen.Kdo.11. A.K. | | FG Trupp a (mot) 411 | 2.8.43 |
| Gen.Kdo.11. A.K. | | FG Trupp 811 | 9.9.43 |
| Gen.Kdo.11. A.K. | | FG Trupp 821 | 9.9.43 |

| | | |
|---|---|---|
| Gen.Kdo.11. A.K. | FG Trupp 831 | 9.9.43 |
| Gen.Kdo.11. A.K. | FG Trupp 836 | 9.9.43 |
| Gen.Kdo.11. A.K. | FG Trupp 851 | 9.9.43 |
| Gen.Kdo.11. A.K. | FG Trupp 852 | 9.9.43 |
| Gen.Kdo.12. A.K. | O.K.II/661/FG | 17.10.39 |
| Gen.Kdo.12. A.K. | Stab, FG Abt 551 | 1.4.41 |
| Gen.Kdo.13. A.K. (Nuernberg) | F.K. 568/FG | 12.9.39 |
| Gen.Kdo.16. A.K. | FG Trupp c (tmot) 1416 | 30.10.44 |
| Gen.Kdo.18. A.K. | Stab, FG Abt (mot) 501 | 1.7.41 |
| Gen.Kdo.18. A.K. | 3.Kp. FG Abt (mot) 501 | 1.7.41 |
| Gen.Kdo.19. (Gebirgs) A.K. | FG Trupp 419 | 22.10.44 |
| Gen.Kdo.20. A.K. | Stab, FG Abt 551 | 19.4.41 |
| Gen.Kdo.23. A.K. | FG Trupp 584 | 8.1.40 |
| Gen.Kdo.25. A.K. | Stab, FG Abt 551 | 25.7.40 |
| Gen.Kdo.27. A.K. | FG Trupp a (mot) 427 | 27.8.39 |
| Gen.Kdo.28. A.K. | FG Trupp a (mot) 428 | 20.5.40 |
| Gen.Kdo.29. A.K. | FG Trupp a 429 | 22.5.40 |
| Gen.Kdo.30. A.K. z.b.V. | FG Trupp c (tmot) 430 | 22.12.44 |
| Gen.Kdo.35. A.K. z.b.V. | FG Trupp b (mot) 88 | 21.7.44 |
| Gen.Kdo.39. A.K. (mot) | Stab, 1.u.2.Kp., FG Abt 551 | 1.6.41 |
| Gen.Kdo.40. A.K. | FG Trupp a (mot) 440 | 27.1.40 |
| Gen.Kdo.40. A.K. | FG Trupp b (mot) 440 | 12.8.40 |
| Gen.Kdo.40. A.K. | 1.Kp. FG Abt (mot) 501 | 1.9.40 |
| Gen.Kdo.40. A.K. | Stab, 1.u.2.Kp., FG Abt 551 | 1.9.41 |
| Gen.Kdo.40. A.K. (Wien) | 2.Kp. FG Abt (mot) 501 | 1.9.40 |
| Gen.Kdo.40. A.K. (Wien) | 3.Kp. FG Abt (mot) 501 | 1.9.40 |
| Gen.Kdo.40. A.K. (Wien) | Stab, FG Abt (mot) 501 | 1.9.40 |
| Gen.Kdo.47. Panzer Kps. | FG Trupp a (mot) 447 | 28.3.44 |
| Gen.Kdo.56. A.K. (mot) | FG Trupp b (mot) 456 | 15.2.41 |
| Gen.Kdo.57. A.K. | 3.Kp.u.1.Zg.2.Kp., FG Abt 551 | 1.6.41 |
| Gen.Kdo.58. Panzer Kps. | FG Trupp b (mot) 458 | 3.11.44 |
| Gen.Kdo.63. A.K. | FG Trupp c (tmot) 1463 | 14.11.44 |
| Gen.Kdo.64. A.K. | FG Trupp a (mot) 464 | 3.11.44 |
| Gen.Kdo.65. A.K. z.b.V. | FG Trupp d 465 | 7.3.44 |
| Gen.Kdo.68. A.K. z.b.V. | FG Trupp z.b.V. 468 | 9.4.43 |
| Gen.Kdo.68. A.K. z.b.V. | FG Trupp b (mot) 468 | 7.10.43 |
| Gen.Kdo.71. A.K. | FG Trupp (mot) 230 | 15.2.43 |
| Gen.Kdo.71. A.K. | FG Trupp (mot) 930 | 5.43 |
| Gen.Kdo.71. A.K. | FG Trupp c (tmot) 630 | 3.6.43 |
| Gen.Kdo.72. A.K. | FG Trupp c (tmot) 472 | 21.11.44 |
| Gen.Kdo.74. A.K. | FG Trupp a (mot) 474 | 21.7.43 |
| Gen.Kdo.75. A.K. z.b.V. | FG Trupp a (mot) 475 | 15.4.44 |
| Gen.Kdo.85. A.K. | FG Trupp a (mot) 485 | 3.11.44 |
| Gen.Kdo.91. A.K. | FG Trupp c (tmot) 491 | 2.11.44 |
| Gen.Kdo.97. A.K. | FG Trupp 487 | 14.12.43 |
| Gen.Kdo.Deutsches Afrikakorps | FG Trupp (mot) 498 | 14.7.41 |

**Generalkommando Kavalleriekorps (Corps Headquarters, Cavalry Corps)**

| | | |
|---|---|---|
| Gen.Kdo.Kav.Kps. | FG Trupp 478 | 25.5.44 |

**Uebergeneralkommando des 21. Armeekorps (Senior Corps Headquarters of the 21st Army Corps)**

| | | |
|---|---|---|
| Ueber.Gen.Kdo.des 21. A.K. | FG Trupp (mot) 442 | 16.8.39 |
| Ueber.Gen.Kdo.des 21. A.K. | FG Trupp (mot) 463 | 26.1.40 |

**Hoehererkommando (Senior Corps Headquarters)**

| | | |
|---|---|---|
| Hoeh.Kdo.33. | Stab, FG Abt 551 | 13.7.40 |

| | | |
|---|---|---|
| Hoeh.Kdo.36. | FG Trupp (mot) 314 | ? |
| Hoeh.Kd.36. | FG Trupp (mot) 436 | 1.4.40 |
| Hoeh.Kdo.45. | FG Trupp (mot) 317 | 24.5.40 |
| Hoeh.Kdo.59. | FG Trupp (Hoeh.Kdo.z.b.V.59.) 459 | 25.10.40 |
| Hoeh.Kdo.z.b.V. 30. A.K. | 3.Kp. FG Abt (mot) 501 | 28.11.39 |
| Hoeh.Kdo.z.b.V. 31. A.K. | FG Trupp a (mot) G 1 | 26.8.39 |
| Hoeh.Kdo.z.b.V. 31. A.K. | FG Trupp 31 | 29.8.39 |
| Hoeh.Kdo.z.b.V. 31. A.K. | 1.Kp. FG Abt (mot) 501 | 28.11.39 |
| Hoeh.Kdo.z.b.V. 31. A.K. | 2.Kp. FG Abt (mot) 501 | 28.11.39 |
| Hoeh.Kdo.z.b.V. 31. A.K. | FG Trupp G 1 | 26.2.40 |
| Hoeh.Kdo.z.b.V. 31. A.K. | FG Trupp 431 | 1.4.40 |
| Hoeh.Kdo.z.b.V. 32. A.K. | FG Trupp 32 (G 2) | 15.10.39 |
| Hoeh.Kdo.z.b.V. 32. A.K. | FG Trupp 432 | 1.4.40 |
| Hoeh.Kdo.z.b.V. 35. A.K. | FG Trupp (mot) 313 | 15.10.39 |
| Hoeh.Kdo.z.b.V. 35. A.K. | FG Trupp (mot) 435 | 1.4.40 |
| Hoeh.Kdo.z.b.V. 37. | O.K. I/594 FG | 3.3.40 |
| Hoeh.Kdo.z.b.V. 37. A.K. | FG Trupp (mot) 330 | 26.10.39 |
| Hoeh.Kdo.z.b.V. 37. A.K. | FG Trupp (mot) 437 | 1.4.40 |

**Luftwaffe Feldkorps (Air Force Field Corps)**

| | | |
|---|---|---|
| 3. Luftwaffe Feldkorps | FG Trupp c (tmot) 63 | 3.8.43 |
| 4. Luftwaffe Feldkorps | FG Trupp c (tmot) 64 | 3.8.43 |

**Reservekorps (Reserve Corps)**

| | | |
|---|---|---|
| 64. Res.Korps | FG Trupp c (tmot) 355 | 25.2.43 |
| 66. Res.Korps | FG Gruppe 466 | 15.5.44 |
| 66. Res.Korps | FG Trupp d (tmot) 466 | 20.6.44 |
| 67. Res.Korps | FG Trupp c (tmot) 357 | 17.3.43 |
| 67. Res.Korps | FG Trupp a (mot) 357 | 21.7.43 |

## REGIMENTS

**Kraftwagentransport Regiment (Motor Transport Regiment)**

| | | |
|---|---|---|
| Kw.Trsp.Rgt.602 | FG Trupp a (mot) 602 | 26.8.39 |
| Kw.Trsp.Rgt.605 | FG Trupp a (mot) 605 | 16.8.39 |
| Kw.Trsp.Rgts.Stab 981 | FG Trupp a (mot) 981 | 20.7.42 |
| Kw.Trsp.Rgts.Stab 982 | FG Trupp a (mot) 982 | 20.7.42 |
| Kw.Trsp.Rgts.Stab z.b.V. 984 | FG Trupp a (mot) 984 | 27.7.42 |

## TRUPPS

**Heerestrupps (Army Troops)**

| | | |
|---|---|---|
| Heerestrupps | FG Trupp 431 | ? |
| Heerestrupps | FG Trupp 309 | 25.8.30 |
| Heerestrupps | Stab, FG Abt (mot) 531 | 2.8.39 |
| Heerestrupps | 1.Kp. FG Abt (mot) 531 | 2.8.39 |
| Heerestrupps | 2.Kp. FG Abt (mot) 531 | 2.8.39 |
| Heerestrupps | 3.Kp. FG Abt (mot) 531 | 2.8.39 |
| Heerestrupps | O.K.II/547 FG Gruppe | 15.8.39 |
| Heerestrupps | Stab, FG Abt (mot) 541 | 16.8.39 |
| Heerestrupps | FG Abt (mot) 685 (mit 1,2,3 Kp) | 19.8.39 |
| Heerestrupps | FG Trupp a (mot) 616 | 25.8.39 |
| Heerestrupps | FG Abt 682 (mit drei Kpn) | 25.8.39 |
| Heerestrupps | Stab, FG Abt (mot) 571 | 26.8.39 |
| Heerestrupps | 1.Kp. FG Abt (mot) 571 | 26.8.39 |
| Heerestrupps | 2.Kp. FG Abt (mot) 571 | 26.8.39 |
| Heerestrupps | 3.Kp. FG Abt (mot) 571 | 26.8.39 |
| Heerestrupps | O.K.II/577 FG | 26.8.39 |

| | | |
|---|---|---|
| Heerestrupps | FG Trupp 582 der O.K.I/582 | 26.8.39 |
| Heerestrupps | Stab, FG Abt (mot) 591 | 26.8.39 |
| Heerestrupps | 1.Kp. FG Abt (mot) 591 | 26.8.39 |
| Heerestrupps | 2.Kp. FG Abt (mot) 591 | 26.8.39 |
| Heerestrupps | 3.Kp. FG Abt (mot) 591 | 26.8.39 |
| Heerestrupps | O.K.II/656 FG | 15.10.39 |
| Heerestrupps | FG Abt (mot) 689 | 6.1.41 |
| Heerestrupps | 1.Kp. FG Abt (mot) 689 | 6.1.41 |
| Heerestrupps | 2.Kp. FG Abt (mot) 689 | 6.1.41 |
| Heerestrupps | 3.Kp. FG Abt (mot) 689 | 6.1.41 |
| Heerestrupps | FG Trupp a (mot) 452 | 15.1.41 |
| Heerestrupps | Stab, FG Abt (mot) 691 | 3.2.41 |
| Heerestrupps | 1.Kp. FG Abt (mot) 691 | 3.2.41 |
| Heerestrupps | 2.Kp. FG Abt (mot) 691 | 3.2.41 |
| Heerestrupps | 3.Kp. FG Abt (mot) 691 | 3.2.41 |
| Heerestrupps | Stab, FG Abt (mot) 694 | 20.3.41 |
| Heerestrupps | 1.Kp. FG Abt (mot) 694 | 20.3.41 |
| Heerestrupps | 2.Kp. FG Abt (mo) 694 | 20.3.41 |
| Heerestrupps | 3.Kp. FG Abt (mot) 694 | 20.3.41 |
| Heerestrupps | FG Abt (mot) 693 | 24.3.41 |
| Heerestrupps | FG Abt (mot) 695 (Stab u.3 Kp.) | 2.5.41 |
| Heerestrupps | FG Trupp d 54 | 17.8.41 |
| Heerestrupps | FG Trupp d 824 | 27.10.41 |
| Heerestrupps | FG Trupp d 599 der F.K. 599 | 15.11.41 |
| Heerestrupps | FG Trupp a (mot) 900 | 6.5.42 |
| Heerestrupps | FG Trupp a (mot) 287 | 4.8.42 |
| Heerestrupps | FG Trupp a (mot) 23 | 2.11.42 |
| Heerestrupps | FG Gruppe 642 | 13.4.43 |
| Heerestrupps | FG Gruppe 643 | 13.4.43 |
| Heerestrupps | FG Gruppe 644 | 13.4.43 |
| Heerestrupps | FG Gruppe 878 | 24.4.43 |
| Heerestrupps | FG Gruppe 879 | 24.4.43 |
| Heerestrupps | FG Gruppe 959 | 24.4.43 |
| Heerestrupps | FG Gruppe 989 | 24.4.43 |
| Heerestrupps | FG Gruppe 996 | 24.4.43 |
| Heerestrupps | FG Gruppe 997 | 24.4.43 |
| Heerestrupps | FG Trupp d 1116 | 1.8.43 |
| Heerestrupps | FG Trupp der 21.Lw.Felddiv. | 8.11.43 |
| Heerestrupps | FG Trupp a (mot) 1111 | 1.12.43 |
| Heerestrupps | FG Trupp d 502 | 17.1.44 |
| Heerestrupps | FG Trupp d 503 | 17.1.44 |
| Heerestrupps | FG Trupp d 513 | 17.1.44 |
| Heerestrupps | FG Trupp d 519 | 17.1.44 |
| Heerestrupps | FG Trupp d 520 | 17.1.44 |
| Heerestrupps | FG Trupp d 522 | 17.1.44 |
| Heerestrupps | FG Trupp d 523 | 17.1.44 |
| Heerestrupps | FG Trupp d 525 | 17.1.44 |
| Heerestrupps | FG Trupp d 529 | 17.1.44 |
| Heerestrupps | FG Trupp d 530 | 17.1.44 |
| Heerestrupps | FG Trupp d 532 | 17.1.44 |
| Heerestrupps | FG Trupp d 534 | 17.1.44 |
| Heerestrupps | FG Trupp d 535 | 17.1.44 |
| Heerestrupps | FG Trupp d 536 | 17.1.44 |
| Heerestrupps | FG Trupp d 537 | 17.1.44 |

| | | |
|---|---|---|
| Heerestrupps | FG Trupp d 538 | 17.1.44 |
| Heerestrupps | FG Trupp d 546 | 17.1.44 |
| Heerestrupps | FG Trupp d 548 | 17.1.44 |
| Heerestrupps | FG Trupp d 556 | 17.1.44 |
| Heerestrupps | FG Trupp d 557 | 17.1.44 |
| Heerestrupps | FG Trupp d 570 | 17.1.44 |
| Heerestrupps | FG Trupp c (tmot) 873 | 4.5.44 |
| Heerestrupps | FG Trupp 1017 | 27.5.44 |
| Heerestrupps | FG Trupp d (tmot) 466 | 20.6.44 |
| Heerestrupps | Stab, FG Abt (mot) 691 | 23.6.44 |
| Heerestrupps | 1.Kp. FG Abt (mot) 691 | 23.6.44 |
| Heerestrupps | 2.Kp. FG Abt (mot) 691 | 23.6.44 |
| Heerestrupps | 3.Kp. FG Abt (mot) 691 | 23.6.44 |
| Heerestrupps | FG Trupp 1143 | 5.7.44 |
| Heerestrupps | FG Trupp d (tmot) 611 | 2.11.44 |
| Heerestrupps | FG Trupp a (mot) 497 | 4.11.44 |
| Heerestrupps | FG Trupp c (tmot) 1150 | 19.12.44 |
| Heerestrupps (Belgien/N.W.Fr.) | FG Trupp c (tmot) 853 | 15.10.41 |
| Heerestrupps (Heeres Geb.A) | Stab, FG Abt (mot) 698 | 27.7.42 |
| Heerestrupps (Heeres Geb.A) | 1.Kp. FG Abt (mot) 698 | 27.7.42 |
| Heerestrupps (Ostfront) | 4.Kp. FG Abt (mot) 693 | 4.6.42 |
| Heerestrupps (Tropen) | FG Kp. (mot) 613 | 18.2.42 |
| Heerestrupps Boehmen u. Maehren | FG Trupp c (tmot) 9 | 22.11.44 |
| Heerestrupps Brindisi | FG Gruppe Brindisi | 29.11.42 |
| Heerestrupps Danzig | FG Trupp Danziger | ? |
| Heerestrupps Tarent | FG Gruppe Tarent | 19.11.42 |
| Heerestrupps (Ord.Dienste) Sizilien | FG Trupp a (mot) Kdo.Sizilien | 5.6.43 |
| **Korpstrupps (Corps Troops)** | | |
| Korpstrupps | FG Trupp z.b.V. 71 | 10.42 |
| Korpstrupps | FG Trupp (mot) 408 | 19.8.39 |
| Korpstrupps | FG Trupp 307 | 25.8.39 |
| Korpstrpps | Grenz.FG Trupp (mot) 303 | 25.8.39 |
| Korpstrupps | FG Trupp 443 | 2.5.40 |
| Korpstrupps | FG Trupp (mot) 433 | 5.5.40 |
| **Divisiontrupps (Division Troops)** | | |
| Divisiontrupps | FG Trupp (mot) 32 | 2.8.39 |
| Divisiontrupps | FG Trupp (mot) 194 | 24.9.39 |
| Divisiontrupps | FG Trupp (mot) 230 | 15.2.43 |
| Divisiontrupps | FG Trupp (mot) 194 | 17.2.43 |
| Divisiontrupps | FG Trupp (mot) 930 | 5.43 |
| Divisiontrupps | FG Trupp c (tmot) 630 | 3.6.43 |
| Divisiontrupps | FG Trupp c (tmot) 542 | 15.7.44 |

# FELDGENDARMERIE FELDPOST NUMBERS

Another category of documents the author received from Herr Bruen Meyer was a list of Feldpost numbers assigned to Feldgendarmerie detachments. Feldpost was the German military postal service and, comparable to a "Zip-Code", the German Armed Forces assigned a series of numbers (known as Feldpostnummer) to their units for routing the mail. This list, like the other, is incomplete, but it can be very useful to someone who wishes to research a document that bears only a Feldpost number instead of spelling out the unit.

For example; in the first volume of this book the author showed a German military driver's license that bore no unit designation other than "Dienststelle Feldpostnummer 02955Z". If one were to check this number (located in the left hand column of this list), they would find that "02 955 Z" belonged to FG Feld.Ers.Kp 5 (Feldgendarmerie Feld Ersatz Kompanie 5, or Military Police Field Replacement Company 5).

Once again, to avoid confusion, the author has left this list in its original form and, whenever notes were added beyond the unit designation, he has left those there as well. When you see a Roman Numeral followed by a two digit numeral, this seems to be a date (ex., XII 43 would be 12/43, or December 1943). Likewise, place names would seem to be locations where a particular unit used this Feldpost number. Just as in the previous list of Feldgendarmerie units, all German terms and abbreviations can be found at the end of this book.

| Feldpost Number | Unit | |
|---|---|---|
| 00 011 | FG Trupp 100 | (Stalingrad) |
| 00 106 | FG Trupp 29 | |
| L 00 106 | FG Abt 29 | (XII 43) |
| 00 149 | FG Trupp 603 | |
| 00 393 | 1./FG Abt 561 | |
| 00 440 | FG Trupp 84 | |
| 00 481 | Stab, FG Abt 693 | (H.Gr.Nord-Ukraine) |
| 00 553 | Stab, FG Abt 696 | |
| 00 572 | FG Trupp 413 | |
| 00 610 | FG Trupp 81 | |
| 00 663 | FG Trupp 352 | (I.44) |
| 00 838 | FG Trupp 617 | |
| 00 886 | FG Trupp 921 | |
| 01 187 | FG Trupp 206 | (H.Gr.Mitte) |
| 01 205 | FG Trupp 194 | (Stalingrad) |
| 01 225 | FG Trupp 15 | |
| 01 257 | FG Trupp 33 | (mot.Afrika II.43) |
| 01 266 | FG Trupp 294 | |
| 01 402 K | FG Trupp 806 | |
| 01 402 K | FG Trupp 814 | |
| 01 402 P | FG Trupp 832 | |
| 01 402 P | FG Trupp 833 | |
| 01 402 W | FG Trupp 824 | |
| 01 402 A Y | FG Trupp 816 | |
| 01 444 | FG Komp B 3 | |

| | |
|---|---|
| 01 460 | FG Trupp 185 |
| 01 468 | FG Trupp 564 |
| 01 568 | FG Trupp 1044 |
| 01 575 | FG Trupp 1176 |
| 01 599 | FG Komp 613 (Tropen) |
| 01 599 | FG Trupp 613 mot.(V.43) |
| 01 631 | FG Trupp 428 |
| 01 641 | FG Trupp 290 |
| 01 701 | 1/FG Abt 591 |
| 02 104 | FG Trupp 3 |
| 02 171 | FG Trupp 486 |
| 02 212 | Stab, FG Abt 521 |
| 02 261 | FG Trupp 404 (VIII.43) |
| 02 294 | 2/FG Abt 591 |
| 02 351 | FG Trupp 404 (Stalingrad) |
| 02 410 | FG Trupp 14 |
| 02 600 | FG Trupp 119 |
| 02 616 | FG Trupp a 376 (Stalingrad) |
| 02 618 | FG Trupp 307 |
| 02 641 | 1/FG Abt 693 |
| 02 643 | Stab, FG Abt 694 |
| 02 725 | FG Trupp 1088 |
| 02 760 | FG Trupp 429 |
| 02 831 | FG Trupp 1045 |
| 02 886 | FG Trupp 218 |
| 02 904 | FG Trupp 35 |
| 02 955 S | FG Trupp 908 |
| 02 955 W | FG Trupp 562 |
| 02 955 Z | FG Feld.Ers.Kp 5 |
| 03 029 | 3/FG Abt 682 |
| 03 069 F T | FG Trupp 786 |
| 03 236 | FG Trupp 402 |
| 03 450 | FG Trupp 832 |
| 03 486 | 2/FG Abt 693 (H.Gr.Nord-Ukraine) |
| 03 491 | 1/FG Abt 694 |
| 03 557 | Stab u.4/FG Abt 551 |
| 03 604 | FG Trupp 148 |
| 03 803 | FG Trupp 629 |
| 03 818 F | FG Trupp 609 |
| 03 818 H | FG Trupp 860 |
| 03 860 | FG Trupp 419 |
| 03 885 | Rgts Stab, FG Ers.Regt.1 |
| 03 981 | 3/FG Abt 531 |
| 04 071 | FG Trupp 162 |
| 04 080 | FG Trupp 11 |
| 04 092 E | FG Trupp 844 |
| 04 102 D | FG Trupp 902 |
| 04 102 P | FG Trupp 571 |
| 04 102 R | FG Trupp 883 |
| 04 102 S | FG Trupp 704 |
| 04 102 T | FG Trupp 741 |
| 04 102 A B | FG Feld.Ers.Kp 4 |
| 04 138 | FG Kp.b.Auffrischungsstab 16 |
| 04 174 | FG Trupp 304 |

| | | |
|---|---|---|
| 04 248 | FG Trupp 208 | |
| 04 373 | 3/FG Abt 581 | |
| 04 390 | FG Trupp 8 | |
| 04 409 | FG Trupp 1064 | |
| 04 423 | FG Trupp 214 | |
| 04 547 A | FG Trupp 759 | |
| 04 563 | 3/FG Abt 693 | (VIII.42) |
| 04 563 | 3/FG Abt 693 | (H.Gr.Nord-Ukraine) |
| 04 684 | 2/FG Abt 694 | |
| 04 689 | 3/FG Abt 591 | |
| 04 833 | Stab I,Grenad.Btl.FG Ers.Rgt. 1 | |
| 05 010 | FG Trupp 90 | (Afrika) |
| 05 166 | 3/FG Abt 694 | |
| 05 263 | FG Abt 571 | (VIII.43 - Russland) |
| 05 263 | 3/FG Abt 571 | (Stalingrad) |
| 05 445 | FG Trupp 161 | |
| 05 514 | 2/FG Abt 682 | |
| 05 612 H | FG Trupp 775 | |
| 05 628 | FG Trupp 28 | |
| 05 774 | FG Trupp 858 | |
| 05 774 | FG Trupp 875 | |
| 05 818 | FG Trupp 447 | |
| 05 947 | FG Trupp 172 | |
| 05 975 B | FG Trupp 839 | |
| 05 975 C | FG Trupp 850 | |
| 06 042 | Stab/II 1.-3.Kp.FG Ers.Rgt. 1 | |
| 06 197 | 3/FG Abt 541 | (Stalingrad) |
| 06 332 G | FG Trupp 852 | |
| 06 332 H | FG Trupp 840 | |
| 06 332 I | FG Trupp 847 | |
| 06 332 K | FG Trupp 855 | |
| 06 332 A B | FG Trupp 848 | |
| 06 402 | FG rupp 59 | |
| 06 500 | FG Trupp 246 | |
| 06 730 | FG Trupp 1600 | |
| 06 738 | 2/FG Abt 551 | |
| 06 768 | FG Trupp 156 | |
| 06 780 H | FG Trupp 764 | |
| 06 874 | FG Trupp 9 | |
| 06 918 | FG Trupp 158 | |
| 07 068 | FG Trupp 885 | |
| 07 162 | FG Trupp 559 | |
| 07 241 | FG Trupp 874 | |
| 07 269 | FG Trupp 20 | |
| 07 454 | 1/FG Abt 696 | |
| 07 515 S | FG Trupp 810 | |
| 07 515 S | FG Trupp 811 | |
| 07 515 S | FG Trupp 831 | |
| 07 515 X | FG Trupp 829 | |
| 07 519 | O.K.I/401 | |
| 07 555 | FG Trupp 1 750 | |
| 07 709 | FG Trupp 17 | |
| 07 716 | FG Trupp 245 | |
| 07 978 | FG Trupp 54 | |

| | | |
|---|---|---|
| 08 080 P | FG Trupp 627 | |
| 08 215 | FG Trupp 309 | |
| 08 309 | FG Trupp 932 | |
| 08 390 | FG Trupp 448 | |
| 08 599 H | FG Trupp 669 | |
| 08 726 | 2/FG Abt 696 | |
| 08 797 A | FG Trupp 818 | |
| 08 824 | FG Trupp 646 | |
| 08 925 | FG Trupp 712 | |
| 09 137 | FG Trupp 565 | |
| 09 186 C | FG Trupp 777 | |
| 09 197 | Stab, FG Abt 591 | |
| 09 399 | FG Trupp 198 | (H.Gr.Nord-Ukraine) |
| 09 423 | FG Trupp 373 | (Kroatien) |
| 09 486 | Royan (I.44) | (Frankreich) |
| 09 487 | FG Trupp 648 | |
| 09 597 | 3/FG Abt 696 | |
| 09 664 H | FG Trupp 774 | |
| 09 664 K | FG Trupp 789 | |
| 09 669 | FG Trupp 754 | (IV.43 Frankreich) |
| 09 712 | FG Trupp 414 | (Stalingrad) |
| 09 831 | FG Trupp 12 | |
| 09 881 | FG Komp. 757 | |
| 09 911 | FG Trupp 357 | |
| 10 002 | FG Trupp 842 | |
| 10 016 | FG Trupp 27 | |
| 10 040 | FG Trupp 654 | |
| 10 097 | 2/FG Abt 581 | |
| 10 160 B | FG Trupp 828 | |
| 10 228 | FG Trupp 465 | |
| 10 255 | FG Trupp 22 | |
| 10 373 | FG Trupp 1901 | |
| 10 479 | FG Trupp 819 | |
| 10 479 | FG Trupp 821 | |
| 10 479 | FG Trupp 835 | |
| 10 546 | 1/FG Abt 521 | |
| 10 713 | FG Trupp 647 | |
| 10 748 U | FG Trupp 986 | |
| 10 748 A.K. | FG Trupp 653 | |
| 10 780 | FG Trupp 436 | |
| 10 822 | FG Trupp 403 | |
| 10 981 | FG Trupp 14 | |
| 11 136 | FG Trupp 650 | |
| 11 228 E | FG Trupp 722 | |
| 11 228 N | FG Trupp 866 | |
| 11 254 | FG Trupp 277 | |
| 11 635 | FG Trupp 392 | (Kroatien) |
| 11 644 A | FG Trupp 808 | |
| 11 645 | Stab, FG Abt 698 | |
| 11 750 K | FG Trupp 791 | |
| 11 971 | FG Trupp 83 | |
| 12 050 | 2/FG Abt 521 | |
| 12 112 | FG Trupp 430 | |
| 12 217 | FG Trupp 676 | |

| | | |
|---|---|---|
| 12 221 | FG Trupp 24 | |
| 12 272 | FG Trupp 529 | (X.42) |
| 12 342 | FG Trupp 571 | |
| 12 368 | FG Trupp 348 | |
| 12 381 | FG Trupp 331 | |
| 12 570 | FG Trupp 475 | |
| 12 641 | FG Trupp 66 | |
| 12 709 | FG Trupp 412 | (H.Gr.Mitte) |
| 12 760 | FG Abt 501 | (I.43 Athen) |
| 12 760 | 3/FG Abt 501 | |
| 12 884 | FG Trupp 302 | |
| 12 974 | 1/FG Abt 501 | |
| 12 998 V | FG Trupp Jonzec | |
| 12 998 A B | FG Trupp 539 | |
| 12 998 A C | FG Trupp 734 | |
| 13 135 | FG Trupp 361 | (H.Gr.Nord-Ukraine) |
| 13 301 | FG Trupp 734 | |
| 13 310 | FG Trupp 150 | (H.Gr.Nord-Ukraine) |
| 13 613 | FG Trupp 6 | (H.Gr.Mitte) |
| 13 70 | FG Trupp 459 | |
| 13 852 | FG Trupp 389 | (Stalingrad) |
| 13 878 | FG Trupp 173 | (H.Gr.Nord-Ukraine) |
| 13 970 | FG Trupp 21 | |
| 14 022 B | FG Trupp 745 | |
| 14 052 | FG Trupp 408 | (Stalingrad) |
| 14 265 | FG Trupp 1 | |
| 14 379 | FG Trupp 81 | |
| 14 413 A D | FG Trupp 972 | |
| 14 415 A S | FG Trupp 695 | |
| 14 812 | 2/FG Abt 541 | (Stalingrad) |
| 15 002 | FG Trupp 7 | |
| 15 047 | FG Trupp 337 | (H.Gr.Mitte) |
| 15 096 | FG Trupp 93 | |
| 15 129 | FG Trupp 69 | |
| 15 169 | FG Trupp 999 (mot) | |
| 15 177 | FG Feld.Ers.Kp. 7 | |
| 15 177 A P | FG Trupp 594 | |
| 15 199 | FG Trupp 217 | |
| 15 199 | FG Trupp 347 | |
| 15 232 G | FG Trupp 822 | |
| 15 232 G | FG Trupp 845 | |
| 15 270 | FG Trupp 417 | |
| 15 321 | FG Trupp 179 | (Stalingrad) |
| 15 515 B | FG Trupp 543 | |
| 15 515 D | FG Trupp 781 | |
| 15 600 | 1/FG Abt 531 | |
| 15 942 | 2/FG Abt 571 | (Stalingrad) |
| 16 076 | FG Trupp 337 | |
| 16 114 | FG Trupp 853 | |
| 16 209 A D | FG Trupp 794 | |
| 16 209 A E | FG Trupp 872 | |
| 16 253 | FG Trupp 169 | |
| 16 280 | Kdo.6.Gren.Div.u.FG Trupp 6 | |
| 16 282 | FG Trupp 170 | |

| | |
|---|---|
| 16 325 | Kdo.545.Volks-grenad.Div.FG Trupp 1545 |
| 16 431 | FG Gruppe 642    (XI.43) |
| 16 431 | FG Trupp 642 |
| 16 578 | 2/FG Abt 561 |
| 16 946 | FG Trupp 353 (mot)  (IV.44) |
| 16 952 | FG Trupp 672 |
| 16 990 | FG Trupp 340 |
| 16 994 | FG Trupp 406 |
| 17 133 | FG Trupp 687 |
| 17 138 | FG Trupp 13 |
| 17 167 | Stab, FG Abt 581 |
| 17 221 | FG Trupp 837 |
| 17 223 | FG Trupp 257       (H.Gr.Mitte) |
| 17 340 | FG Trupp 129 |
| 17 502 | FG Trupp 220       (Afrika) |
| 17 502 | FG Trupp 485 |
| 17 502 | FG Trupp 652 |
| 17 527 | FG Trupp 19 |
| 17 632 | Stabsoffiziere der FG in Daenemark |
| 17 090 | FG Trupp 864 |
| 17 730 | FG Trupp 152 |
| 17 813 | FG Trupp 666 |
| 17 842 | FG Trupp 1124 |
| 17 847 | FG Trupp 606 |
| 17 880 | FG Trupp 303 |
| 17 881 | FG Trupp 612 |
| 17 881 | Gen.Kdo.Korps Oder |
| 17 889 | Stab, FG Abt 501 |
| 17 930 | FG Trupp 212 |
| 17 943 A C | FG Trupp 626 |
| 18 129 H | FG Trupp 751 |
| 18 191 | FG Trupp 910 |
| 18 274 | FG Trupp 432 |
| 18 309 | Kdo.560.Volks-Gren.Div. FG Trupp 1560 |
| 18 312 | FG Trupp 1125 |
| 18 447 | FG Trupp Kdo. 192(XII.44) Heimkehrer |
| 18 450 | FG Trupp 276 |
| 18 523 | FG Trupp 1049 |
| 18 541 | FG Trupp 264 |
| 18 606 | FG Trupp 665 |
| 18 606 F | FG Trupp 744 |
| 18 606 G | FG Trupp 655 |
| 18 753 | FG Trupp 278 |
| 18 812 | FG Trupp 690 |
| 18 900 | FG Trupp 256 |
| 18 902 | 1/FG Abt 581 |
| 18 972 | FG Trupp 662 |
| 19 259 | FG Trupp 31         (H.Gr.Mitte) |
| 19 358 | FG Trupp 178       (H.Gr.Mitte) |
| 19 393 | FG Komp. B 7 |
| 19 426 | FG Trupp 435       (H.Gr.Mitte) |
| 19 580 | Div.Kdo.36.Volks-Gren.Div.u.FG Trupp 36 |
| 19 678 | FG Trupp 30 |
| 19 744 | FG Trupp 405 |

| | | |
|---|---|---|
| 19 757 | FG Trupp 3 | (Stalingrad) |
| 19 938 | FG Trupp 957 | |
| 20 008 | Kdo.549.Volks-Gren.Div.u.FG Trupp 1549 | |
| 20 012 | FG Trupp 110 | (H.Gr.Mitte) |
| 20 075 | 3/FG Abt 521 | |
| 20 130 | Kdo.544.Volks-Gren.Div.u.FG Trupp 1544 | |
| 20 172 | FG Trupp 177 (mot) (1944) | |
| 20 275 E | FG Trupp 729 | |
| 20 365 | 1/FG Abt 541 | (Stalingrad) |
| 20 380 | FG Trupp 708 | |
| 20 445 | FG Trupp 931 | |
| 20 644 | Stab, FG Abt 697 | |
| 20 710 | Stab, FG Abt 561 | |
| 20 750 | FG Trupp 10 | |
| 20 752 | FG Trupp 32 | |
| 20 778 | FG Trupp 282 | |
| 21 041 | FG Trupp 408 | |
| 21 218 | FG Trupp 437 | |
| 21 241 | FG Trupp 306 | (VIII.43 Russland) |
| 21 251 | FG Trupp 369 | |
| 21 430 | FG Trupp 754 | |
| 21 665 | FG Trupp 689 | |
| 21 740 A B | FG Trupp 506 | |
| 21 749 | 1/FG Abt 697 | |
| 21 872 | FG Trupp 5 | |
| 22 127 | FG Trupp 1115d | |
| 22 170 | Kdo.551.Volks-Gren.Div.FG Trupp 1551 | |
| 22 258 | FG Trupp 356 | |
| 22 325 | FG Trupp 26 | |
| 22 371 | Stab, FG Abt 531 | |
| 22 372 | 2/FG Abt 531 | |
| 22 501 E | FG Trupp 641 | |
| 22 640 | FG Trupp 659 | |
| 22 537 | FG Abt 697 | (VIII.4 Russland) |
| 22 537 | 2/FG Abt 697 | |
| 22 627 | FG Trupp 670 | |
| 22 688 A | FG Gruppe 990 | |
| 22 688 H | FG Gruppe 997 | |
| 22 700 | 3/FG Abt 561 | |
| 22 785 | FG Trupp 1541 | |
| 22 785 | Kdo.Tross u.Kampfschule.541.Vo.Gr.u.1841 | |
| 22 822 | FG Trupp d 960 | |
| 22 843 | FG Trupp 433 | |
| 22 854 | Kdo.275.Vo.Gr.Div.u.FG Trupp 275 | |
| 22 861 | FG Trupp 926 | |
| 22 874 | Stab, FG Abt 682 | |
| 22 940 | FG Trupp 187 | |
| 22 960 | FG Trupp 411 | (Stalingrad) |
| 23 032 G | FG Gruppe 996 | |
| 23 111 | FG Trupp 496 | |
| 23 241 | FG Trupp 685 | |
| 23 259 | FG Trupp 34 | |
| 23 310 | FG Trupp 272 | |
| 23 398 | 3/FG Abt 697 | |

| | | |
|---|---|---|
| 23 424 | FG Trupp 44 | (Stalingrad) |
| 23 504 | FG Trupp z.b.V. AOK Norwegen | |
| 23 800 | FG Trupp 235 | |
| 23 850 | FG Trupp 361 | |
| 23 920 | FG Trupp 526 | |
| 23 936 A A | FG Trupp 502 | |
| 24 210 | FG Trupp 31 | |
| 24 258 | FG Gruppe 878 | |
| 24 258 | FG Trupp 989 | |
| 24 258 R | FG Trupp 879 | |
| 24 258 S | FG Gruppe 959 | |
| 24 282 | Kdo.78.Volkssturm.Div.u.FG Trupp 178 | |
| 24 289 | FG Trupp 190 | (Afrika) |
| 24 368 | FG Trupp 4 | (Stalingrad) |
| 24 411 | FG Trupp 175 | |
| 24 418 | FG Trupp 230 | |
| 24 441 | Stab, FG Abt 571 | |
| 24 634 | FG Trupp 317 | |
| 24 638 | FG Trupp 1058 | |
| 24 703 | Stab, FG Abt 541 (Stalingrad) | |
| 24 705 | FG Trupp 171 | (Stalingrad) |
| 24 830 | FG Trupp 326 | |
| 24 895 | 2/FG Abt 501 | |
| 25 007 | FG Trupp 431 | |
| 25 024 | FG Trupp 241 | |
| 25 115 | FG Trupp 263 | |
| 25 228 | FG Trupp 208 | |
| 25 254 | FG Trupp 616 | |
| 25 374 | FG Trupp 36 | (H.Gr.Mitte) |
| 25 600 | FG Trupp 340 | (H.Gr.Nord-Ukraine) |
| 25 619 | FG Trupp 468 | |
| 25 629 | 1/FG Abt 682 | |
| 25 749 | FG Trupp 900 | |
| 25 750 | FG Trupp 219 | |
| 25 795 F | FG Trupp 629 | |
| 26 033 A E | FG Trupp 604 | (II.44) |
| 26 046 | FG Kdo.Grohd. Feldjaeger Rgt. 3 | |
| 26 065 | FG Trupp 663 | |
| 26 139 | FG Trupp 409 | |
| 26 142 | FG Trupp 405 | (H.Gr.Nord-Ukraine) |
| 26 366 | FG Trupp 443 | |
| 26 377 | FG Trupp 401 | |
| 26 397 | FG Trupp 909 | |
| 26 443 | FG Trupp 610 | |
| 26 458 | FG Trupp 458 | |
| 26 458 | FG Trupp 688 | |
| 26 460 | FG Trupp 1 | |
| 26 463 | FG Trupp 911 | |
| 26 508 | FG Trupp 1903 | |
| 26 538 | FG Trupp 854 (mot) | (I.44, Luxembg.) |
| 26 624 | 3/FG Abt 551 | |
| 26 641 | Stab, FG Abt 695 | |
| 26 641 | Ostkomp. 613 | |
| 26 786 | FG Trupp 1128 | |

| | | |
|---|---|---|
| 26 843 S | FG Trupp 550 | |
| 26 843 T | FG Trupp 622 | |
| 26 843 U | FG Trupp 660 | |
| 26 843 V | FG Trupp 721 | |
| 26 854 | FG Trupp 849 | |
| 26 867 | FG Trupp 18 | (H.Gr.Mitte) |
| 26 948 | FG Trupp 727 | |
| 26 952 | FG Trupp 164 | |
| 26 975 | FG Trupp 67 | |
| 27 021 | 1/FG Abt 695 | |
| 27 284 | FG Trupp 60 | |
| 27 348 | FG Trupp 2901 | |
| 27 364 | FG Trupp 234 | |
| 27 519 Z | FG Trupp 785 | |
| 27 549 | 2/FG Abt 695 | |
| 27 638 | FG Trupp 630 | |
| 27 701 | FG Trupp 176 | (Stalingrad) |
| 27 953 | FG Trupp 16 | (Stalingrad) |
| 27 964 | 3/FG Abt 695 | |
| 28 021 | FG Trupp 2902 | |
| 28 023 | FG Trupp 1902 | |
| 28 110 | FG Komp. 914 | |
| 28 316 | FG Trupp 246 | |
| 28 400 | Kdo.548.Vo.Grn.Div.FG Trupp 1548 | |
| 28 408 | FG Trupp 95 | |
| 28 500 | FG Trupp d 1091 | |
| 28 557 | FG Trupp 2903 | |
| 28 662 | FG Trupp 10 | |
| 28 695 | FG Trupp 58 | |
| 28 697 | FG Trupp 25 | (H.Gr.Mitte) |
| 28 762 | FG Trupp 671 | |
| 28 878 | FG Trupp 45 | (H.Gr.Mitte) |
| 29 082 | FG Trupp 213 | |
| 29 213 F | FG Trupp 549 | |
| 29 213 Z | FG Trupp 542 | |
| 29 266 | FG Trupp 168 | |
| 29 297 | FG Trupp 823 | |
| 29 363 | FG Trupp 460 F | (XII.43) |
| 29 378 | FG Trupp 347 | |
| 29 550 | FG Trupp 2 | |
| 29 750 | FG Trupp 352 | |
| 29 828 | FG Trupp 3901 | |
| 29 870 | FG Trupp 179 | |
| 29 900 | FG Trupp 147 | |
| 29 915 | 1/FG Abt 551 | |
| 29 992 | FG Trupp 29 | (Stalingrad) |
| 29 993 | FG Trupp 424 | |
| 30 008 | FG Trupp 195 | |
| 30 008 | FG Trupp 256 | (H.Gr.Mitte) |
| 30 019 | FG Trupp 446 | |
| 30 040 | FG Trupp 836 | |
| 30 441 | FG Komp.LIII A.K.(H.Gr.Mitte) | |
| 30 467 | FG Trupp 3902 | |
| 30 607 | FG Komp.904 (mot)(III.4, Kreta) | |

| | | |
|---|---|---|
| 30 607 | FG Trupp 133 | |
| 30 672 | FG Trupp 1542 | |
| 30 680 | FG Trupp 1561 | |
| 30 860 | FG Trupp 3903 | |
| 30 898 | FG Trupp 232 | |
| 30 999 | FG Trupp 376 | |
| 31 092 | FG Trupp 254 | |
| 31 322 | FG Trupp 410 | |
| 31 329 | FG Trupp 253 | |
| 31 378 | FG Trupp 367 | |
| 31 402 | FG Komp. Grossdeutschland | |
| 31 441 | FG Trupp 550 | |
| 31 477 | FG Trupp 439 (mot) (I.40 i.Osten) | |
| 31 480 | FG Trupp 25 | |
| 31 525 | FG Trupp 196 | |
| 31 606 | FG Trupp 362 | |
| 31 637 | FG Trupp 674 | |
| 31 891 | FG Trupp 233 | |
| 31 916 | FG Trupp 222 | |
| 31 941 | FG Trupp 193 | |
| 31 952 | FG Trupp 219 | (H.Gr.Nord-Ukraine) |
| 32 000 | FG Trupp 868 | |
| 32 200 | FG Trupp 18 | |
| 32 227 | FG Trupp 834 | |
| 32 239 | FG Trupp 840 | |
| 32 499 | FG Trupp 407 | |
| 32 756 | FG Trupp 240 | (X.41) |
| 32 814 | FG Trupp 859 | |
| 32 920 | FG Trupp 84 | |
| 33 015 | FG Trupp 441 | |
| 33 062 | Stab, FG Abt 685 | |
| 33 199 E | FG Trupp 805 | |
| 33 387 | FG Trupp 748 | |
| 33 396 | FG Trupp 44 | |
| 33 477 | FG Trupp 40 | |
| 33 481 | FG Trupp 414 | |
| 33 518 | 1/FG Abt 683 | |
| 33 518 | FG Trupp 756 | |
| 33 564 | FG Trupp 229 | (H.Gr.Mitte) |
| 33 596 | FG Trupp 905 | |
| 33 596 | FG Trupp 998 | |
| 33 614 | FG Trupp 199 | |
| 33 635 | FG Trupp 371 | |
| 33 851 | FG Trupp 82 | (VIII.43, Russland) |
| 33 861 | FG Trupp 82 | (VIII.43, Russland) |
| 33 901 | FG Trupp 57 | |
| 33 997 | FG Trupp 411 | |
| 34 026 | FG Trupp 125 (mot) (H.Gr.Nord-Ukraine) | |
| 34 041 | FG Trupp 171 | (XII.43) |
| 34 159 | 1/FG Abt 698 | |
| 34 306 | FG Trupp 898 | |
| 34 402 | FG Trupp 248 | |
| 34 560 | FG Trupp 319 | |
| 34 651 | 2/FG Abt 685 | |

| 34 746 | FG Trupp 272 | |
|---|---|---|
| 34 753 | 3/FG Abt 685 | |
| 34 829 | FG Trupp 194 | |
| 34 844 | FG Trupp 494 | (X.42) |
| 34 920 | FG Komp. B 5 | |
| 34 921 | FG Trupp 46 | |
| 35 114 | FG Trupp 585 | (XII.41, Tunis) |
| 35 194 | FG Trupp 160 | (Stalingrad) |
| 35 300 | FG Trupp 162 | |
| 35 341 | FG Trupp 114 | |
| 35 478 | FG Trupp 91 | |
| 35 523 | FG Trupp 85 | |
| 35 603 | FG Trupp 104 | |
| 35 735 | 1/FG Abt 683 | (VIII.42) |
| 35 735 | FG Komp. 614 | (Afrika) |
| 35 805 | FG Trupp 87 | |
| 35 868 | FG Trupp 118 | |
| 35 899 | FG Trupp 188 | |
| 36 048 | 3/FG Abt 683 | |
| 36 086 | FG Trupp 867 | |
| 36 101 | FG Trupp 200 | (Afrika) |
| 36 128 | FG Trupp 225 | |
| 36 144 | 2/FG Abt 683 | |
| 36 157 | 4/FG Abt 581 | |
| 36 228 | 1/FG Abt 571 | |
| 36 470 | FG Komp. 675 | (1940) |
| 36 470 | FG Trupp 801 | |
| 36 529 | FG Trupp 176 | |
| 36 578 | FG Trupp 453 | |
| 36 600 | FG Trupp 297 | (Stalingrad) |
| 36 758 | FG Trupp 605 | |
| 36 763 | FG Trupp 1142 | |
| 36 899 | FG Trupp 881 | |
| 36 935 | FG Trupp 131 | |
| 36 995 | FG Trupp 539 | |
| 37 000 | FG Trupp 68 | |
| 37 021 | FG Trupp 70 | |
| 37 021 | FG Trupp 442 | (VII.42) |
| 37 052 | FG Trupp 258 | |
| 37 059 | FG Trupp 269 | |
| 37 085 | FG Trupp 675 | |
| 37 229 | FG Trupp 1547 | |
| 37 316 | 3/FG Abt 698 | |
| 37 420 | FG Trupp 292 | |
| 37 485 | FG Trupp 449 | (H.Gr.Nord-Ukraine) |
| 37 526 | FG Trupp 438 | |
| 37 570 | FG Trupp 387 | |
| 37 646 | FG Trupp 211 | |
| 37 765 | FG Abt 683 | (VII.42) |
| 37 765 | Stab, FG Abt 683 | |
| 37 767 | FG Trupp 444 | |
| 37 842 | FG Trupp 316 | |
| 38 146 | FG Trupp 291 | (VIII.43, Russland) |
| 38 260 | FG Trupp 61 | |

| | | |
|---|---|---|
| 38 340 | FG Trupp 295 | (Stalingrad) |
| 38 448 | FG Trupp 241 | (VIII.43, Russland) |
| 38 500 | FG Trupp 83 | |
| 38 590 | FG Trupp 815 | |
| 38 820 | FG Trupp 251 | |
| 38 822 | FG Trupp 452 | |
| 38 979 | 1/FG Abt 685 | |
| 39 006 | FG Trupp 370 | |
| 39 036 | FG Trupp 477 | |
| 39 071 | FG Trupp 183 | |
| 39 075 | FG Trupp 299 | (H.Gr.Mitte) |
| 39 104 | FG Trupp 195 | 39 182    2/FG Abt 698 |
| 39 219 | FG Trupp 260 | |
| 39 231 | FG Trupp 296 | (H.Gr.Mitte) |
| 39 284 | FG Trupp 132 | |
| 39 295 | FG Trupp 487 | |
| 39 436 | FG Trupp 305 | (Stalingrad) |
| 39 461 | FG Trupp 359 | |
| 39 491 | FG Trupp 165 | |
| 39 511 | FG Trupp 329 | |
| 39 525 | FG Trupp 45 | |
| 39 525 | FG Trupp 1546 | |
| 39 541 | FG Trupp 179 | |
| 39 543 | FG Trupp 252 | |
| 39 598 | FG Trupp 257 | |
| 39 645 | FG Trupp 308 | |
| 39 669 | FG Trupp 371 | (Stalingrad + VIII.43 Russ.) |
| 39 698 | FG Trupp 149 | |
| 39 972 | FG Trupp 181 | |
| 40 063 | Stab, FG Abt 689 | |
| 40 068 | FG Trupp 709 | |
| 40 075 | FG Trupp 719 | |
| 40 093 | Kdo.711.Inf.Div.FG Trupp 711 | |
| 40 174 | FG Staffel 1001 | |
| 40 220 | FG Trupp 277 | |
| 40 243 | FG Trupp 919 | |
| 40 286 | Stab, FG Abt 690 | |
| 40 315 | FG Trupp 1553 | |
| 40 452 | FG Trupp 336 | (H.Gr.Nord-Ukraine) |
| 40 514 | FG Trupp 420 | |
| 40 535 | FG Trupp 457 | |
| 40 651 | FG Trupp Oder-Korps | |
| 41 044 | FG Komp. B 4 | |
| 41 044 | FG Feld.Ers.Komp. 2 | |
| 41 072 | FG Trupp 88 | (VIII.43, Russland) |
| 41 140 | FG Trupp 1562 | |
| 41 177 | 4/FG Abt 619 | |
| 41 198 | Stab, FG Abt 691 | |
| 41 417 | FG Trupp 418 | |
| 41 429 | 1/FG Abt 689 | |
| 41 749 | FG Trupp 159 | |
| 41 933 | FG Trupp 328 | (Sued-Ukraine) |
| 42 004 | 2/FG Abt 619 | |
| 42 131 | FG Trupp 226 | |

| | | |
|---|---|---|
| 42 322 | 2/FG Abt 689 | |
| 42 468 | FG Trupp 297 | |
| 42 505 | FG Trupp 106 | |
| 42 556 | FG Trupp 478 | |
| 42 648 | FG Trupp 416 | |
| 42 708 | FG Trupp 1059 | |
| 42 746 | 1/FG Abt 691 | |
| 42 763 | FG Staffel 1003  (X.43) | |
| 43 035 | FG Trupp 128 | |
| 43 140 | FG Trupp 1558 | |
| 43 189 | FG Trupp 451 | (Stalingrad) |
| 43 228 | FG Feld.Ers.Komp. 1 | |
| 43 264 | 3/FG Abt 690 | |
| 43 333 | FG Trupp 450 | |
| 43 406 F | FG Trupp 826 | |
| 43 568 | 2/FG Abt 691 | |
| 43 663 | FG Trupp 17 | |
| 43 965 | FG Trupp 237 | |
| 43 977 | 3/FG Abt 689 | |
| 44 047 | FG Trupp 101 | |
| 44 315 | FG Trupp 305 | |
| 44 349 | FG Trupp 474 | |
| 44 513 | FG Trupp 384 | |
| 44 524 | Stab, FG Abt 692 | |
| 44 632 | FG Trupp 97 | |
| 44 805 | FG Trupp 356 | |
| 44 914 | FG Trupp 271 | |
| 45 038 | 1/FG Abt 692 | |
| 45 053 | FG Trupp 389 | |
| 45 237 | 3/FG Abt 691 | |
| 45 370 | FG Trupp 244 | |
| 45 736 | FG Trupp 455 | |
| 45 838 | FG Trupp 363 | |
| 46 093 | FG Trupp 935 | |
| 46 114 | FG Trupp 907 | |
| 46 174 | FG Trupp 384 | (Stalingrad) |
| 46 182 | FG Trupp 134 | (H.Gr.Mitte) |
| 46 326 | FG Trupp 377 | |
| 46 284 | FG Trupp 122 | |
| 46 317 | 2/FG Abt 692 | (I.44) |
| 46 328 | FG Trupp 113 | (Stalingrad) |
| 46 569 | FG Trupp 142 | |
| 46 622 | FG Trupp 427 | (H.Gr.Mitte) |
| 46 735 | FG Trupp 456 | |
| 46 960 | FG Trupp 111 | (H.Gr.Nord-Ukraine) |
| 46 964 | FG Trupp 99 | |
| 47 073 | FG Trupp 545 | |
| 47 115 | FG Trupp 92 | |
| 47 123 | FG Trupp 335 | |
| 47 160 | 3/FG Abt 541 | |
| 47 264 | FG Trupp 123 | |
| 47 277 | FG Trupp 112 | |
| 47 380 | FG Trupp 369 | (Kroatien) |
| 47 414 | FG Trupp 126 | |

| | | |
|---|---|---|
| 47 430 | FG Trupp 121 | |
| 47 469 | FG Trupp 462 | |
| 47 473 | FG Trupp 342 | |
| 47 498 | FG Trupp 102 | |
| 47 524 | FG Trupp 344 | |
| 47 524 | FG Trupp 1180 | |
| 47 600 | FG Trupp, Div.Ulrich v. Hutten | |
| 47 609 | FG Trupp 40 | (Stalingrad) |
| 47 653 | FG Trupp 983 | |
| 47 697 | FG Trupp 383 | (H.Gr.Mitte) |
| 47 735 | FG Trupp 16 | |
| 47 886 | 3/FG Abt 692 | |
| 47 960 | FG Trupp 94 | |
| 48 010 | FG Trupp 535 | |
| 48 166 | FG Trupp 23 | |
| 48 432 | FG Trupp 715 | |
| 48 459 | FG Trupp 346 | |
| 48 459 | FG Trupp 999 | (Afrika) |
| 48 470 | FG Trupp 680 | |
| 48 650 | FG Trupp 349 | |
| 48 796 | FG Trupp 338 | |
| 48 837 | FG Trupp 334 | (III.43) |
| 48 887 | FG Trupp 334 | (Afrika) |
| 49 264 | FG Trupp 1117 | |
| 49 309 | FG Trupp 1116 | |
| 49 330 | FG Trupp 63 | |
| 49 645 | FG Trupp 1112 | |
| 50 757 | FG Trupp 1115 | |
| 50 981 | FG Trupp 1114 | |
| 51 063 | FG Trupp 1017 | |
| 51 098 | FG Trupp 1120 | |
| 51 812 | FG Trupp 64 | |
| 54 018 | FG Trupp 1122 | |
| 55 435 | FG Trupp 1000 | |
| 55 466 | FG Trupp 1121 | |
| 56 068 | FG Trupp 467 | |
| 56 311 | FG Trupp 404 | |
| 56 400 | FG Trupp 55 | (1/Kos.Div.) |
| 56 434 A | FG Trupp 820 | |
| 56 453 | FG Trupp 924 | (X.43) |
| 56 454 | FG Trupp 243 | (VI.44) |
| 56 603 | FG Trupp 631 | |
| 56 695 | FG Trupp Venedig | |
| 56 912 | FG Trupp 295 | |
| 56 950 | FG Trupp 1562 | |
| 56 985 | FG Staffel 1006 | |
| 57 014 | FG Trupp 334 | |
| 57 034 | FG Trupp 280 | |
| 57 039 | FG Trupp 242 | |
| 57 147 | FG Trupp 87 | |
| 57 211 | FG Trupp 605 | |
| 57 268 | FG Trupp 1101 | |
| 57 286 | FG Trupp 33 | |
| 57 305 | FG Trupp 702 | |

| | |
|---|---|
| 57 332 | FG Trupp 513 |
| 57 334 | FG Eins.Komp.z.b.V. BDO Italien |
| 57 439 | FG Komp. 236 |
| 57 528 | FG Trupp 100 (mot)  (XI.43, Albanien) |
| 57 599 | FG Trupp 422 |
| 57 736 | FG Trupp 264 |
| 57 740 | FG Trupp 1110 |
| 57 876 | FG Trupp 415 |
| 57 948 | FG Trupp 536 |
| 57 953 | FG Trupp 184 |
| 57 994 | FG Trupp 546 |
| 58 041 | FG Trupp 451 |
| 58 054 | FG Trupp 1103 |
| 58 083 | FG Trupp 476 |
| 58 199 | FG Trupp 537 |
| 58 266 | FG Trupp 4 |
| 58 406 | FG Trupp 512 |
| 58 487 | FG Trupp 189 (mot) (89.Inf.Div., IV.44) |
| 58 595 | FG Trupp 710 |
| 58 735 | FG Trupp 190 |
| 58 891 | FG Trupp 265 |
| 58 894 | FG Trupp 274 |
| 59 140 | FG Trupp 117 |
| 59 193 | FG Trupp 141 (mot) |
| 59 254 | FG Trupp 191 |
| 59 371 | FG Trupp 185 |
| 59 438 | FG Trupp 421 |
| 59 538 | FG Trupp 147 |
| 59 633 | FG Trupp 1109      (H.Gr.Mitte) |
| 59 681 | FG Trupp 1104 |
| 59 709 | FG Trupp 519 |
| 59 721 | FG Trupp 47th A.K. |
| 59 725 | FG Trupp Feldherrnhalle  (H.Gr.Mitte) |
| 59 825 | FG Trupp 554 |
| 64 010 | FG Trupp 167 |
| 64 060 | FG Trupp 7 |
| 64 091 | FG Trupp 857 |
| 64 106 | FG Trupp 942 |
| 64 110 | FG Trupp 82 |
| 64 113 | FG Trupp 589 |
| 64 235 | FG Trupp 901 |
| 64 339 | FG Trupp 817 |
| 64 357 | FG Trupp 611 |
| 64 377 | FG Komp. b.Rhein Kdt. I |
| 64 460 | FG Trupp 540 |
| 64 479 | FG Komp. G 6 |
| 64 569 | FG Trupp 785 |
| 64 872 | FG Komp. G 1 |
| 64 879 | FG Komp. B 1 |
| 64 906 | FG Trupp 947 |
| 64 948 | FG Trupp 837 |
| 64 958 | FG Komp. G 10 |
| 65 030 | FG Trupp 271 |
| 65 094 | FG Trupp 464 |

| | | |
|---|---|---|
| 65 094 | FG Trupp 510 | |
| 65 187 | FG Trupp 769 | |
| 65 287 | FG Trupp 1046 | |
| 65 483 | FG Komp. G 2 | |
| 65 542 | FG Trupp 553 | |
| 65 542 | FG Trupp 901 | |
| 65 553 | FG Komp. G 8 | |
| 65 593 | FG Trupp 1043 | |
| 65 604 | FG Trupp 556 | |
| 65 671 | FG Trupp 568 | |
| 65 726 | FG Komp. B 2 | |
| 65 764 | FG Trupp 1609 | |
| 65 770 | FG Trupp 1036 | |
| 65 878 | FG Trupp 508 | |
| 66 089 | FG Trupp 1047 | |
| 66 095 | FG Trupp 747 | |
| 66 095 | FG Trupp 813 | |
| 66 115 | FG Komp. G 7 | |
| 66 254 | FG Trupp 925 | |
| 66 403 | FG Trupp 894 | |
| 66 403 | FG Trupp 1025 | |
| 66 422 | FG Trupp 491 | |
| 66 544 | FG Trupp 899 | |
| 66 665 | FG Trupp 976 | |
| 66 720 | FG Trupp 215 | |
| 66 815 | FG Trupp 773 | |
| 66 823 | FG Trupp Fuehrer Grenadier Brigade | |
| 67 022 | FG Trupp 1141 | |
| 67 081 | FG Trupp 658 | |
| 67 103 | FG Trupp 1035 | |
| 67 138 | FG Komp. G 3 | |
| 67 322 | FG Trupp 950 | |
| 67 527 | FG Trupp 15 | |
| 67 607 | FG Trupp 608 | |
| 67 647 | FG Trupp 12 | |
| 67 648 | FG Komp. G 5 | |
| 67 658 | FG Komp. G 9 | |
| 67 716 | FG Trupp 585 | |
| 67 770 | FG Trupp 13 | |
| 67 835 | FG Trupp 320 | |
| 68 035 | FG Trupp 133 | (Inselteil) |
| 68 055 | FG Trupp 718 | (Inselteil) |
| 68 055 | FG Trupp 941 | (Inselteil) |
| 80 050 10 | FG Abt d.3.Inf.Div. | |
| 80 050 | FG Trupp 3 | |
| 80 322 | FG Trupp 2 | |
| 80 617 | FG Trupp 4 | |
| 80 454 | FG Trupp 1 | |

# GLOSSARY

| | |
|---|---|
| A.K. | Armee Korps (Army Corps) |
| A.Nachsch.Fueh. | Armee Nachschubfuehrer (Chief of Supply Services, Army) |
| A.O.K. | Armee Oberkommando (Army High Command) |
| Albanien | Albania |
| alten | old |
| Armee | Army (tactical unit) |
| Artillerie | Artillery |
| Ausbildungs | Training |
| Bandenjaeger | Partisan Hunters |
| Befh. | Befehlshaber (Commander) |
| Begleit | Escort |
| Behelfsmaessiger | auxiliary |
| Bez. | Bezirk (District) |
| Bezirk | District |
| Boehmen-Maehren | Bohemia-Moravia |
| Daenemark | Denmark |
| der | "the", or "of the" |
| des | "of the" |
| Deutsche | German |
| Dienststelle | Duty Station |
| Div. | Division |
| Div. Trupps | Division Troops |
| Eins. | Einsatz (Employment) |
| Ersatz | Replacement |
| Ev.-luth. | Evangelisch-lutherisch (Lutheran) |
| F. | Feld (Field) |
| F.K. | Feldkommandantur (Military Administration Headquarters -Field) |
| Fallschirmjaeger | Paratrooper |
| Feld | Field |
| Feldgendarm | Individual Military Policeman |
| Feldgendarmen | Military Policemen |
| Feldgendarmerie | Military Police |
| Feldkorps | Field Corps |
| Feldwebel | Sergeant First Class |
| Festung | Fortress |
| FG | Feldgendarmerie (Military Police) |
| FG Abt | Feldgendarmerie Abteilung (Military Police Battalion) |
| FG AusbAbt | Feldgendarmerie Ausbildungs Abteilung (Military Police Training Battalion) |
| Fliegerkorps | Air Force Corps |
| Fr. | Frankreich (France) |
| Fuer | For |
| Geb. | Gebiet (Zone) |
| Gebeit | Zone |
| Gebirgs | Mountain |
| Gefreiter | Lance Corporal |

| | |
|---|---|
| Gen.Kdo. | General Kommando (Corps Headquarters) |
| Generalgouvernement | General Government |
| Gr. | Grenadier |
| Grenadier | Variation of Infantry |
| Grenz | Frontier |
| Grenzschutz | Frontier Defense |
| Gross | Greater |
| Gruppe | Group (tactical unit) |
| Grz. | Grenz (Frontier) |
| Hauptfeldwebel | First Sergeant |
| Heeres | Army |
| Heeres Trupps | Army Troops |
| Hoeh.Kdo. | Hoehere Kommando (Senior |
| i. | in, or in the |
| Infanterie | Infantry |
| Inselteil Island | Unit |
| Italien | Italian |
| Jaeger | Literally "Hunter", but can be translated to read "rifle" as in Jaeger Division (Rifle Division) |
| Jg. | Jaeger (See Jaeger) |
| K.K. | Kreiskommandantur (Area Headquarters - Military Government) |
| Kampfschule | War School |
| Kath. | Katholisch (Catholic) |
| Kavallerie | Cavalry |
| Kdo. | Kommando (Command) |
| Kdt. | Kommandant (Commanding Officer) |
| Kettenhunde | Chain Dogs |
| Kopenhagen | Copenhagen |
| Korps | Corps |
| Korueck | Kommandant Rueckwaertige (Commanding Officer, Rear Area) |
| Kos.Div. | Kossak Division (Cossack Division) |
| Kp. | Kompanie (Company) |
| Kps. | Korps (Corps) |
| Kraftwagentransport regiment | Motor Transport Regiment |
| Krakau | Cracow or Krakow, Poland |
| Kreta | Crete |
| Kroatien | Croatian |
| Kw.Trsp.Rgt. | Kraftwagentransportregiment (Motor Transport Regiment) |
| L.P. | Landespolizei (Regional Police) |
| Ldw.Div. | Landwehr Division -Reserve Division |
| Le. | Leichte (Light) |
| Lehrbrigade | Training Brigade |
| Leichte | Light |
| Luftwaffe | Air Force |
| Lw. | Luftwaffe (Air Force) |
| Mil.Befh. | Militaer Befehlshaber (Military Commander) |

| | |
|---|---|
| Mil.Kdtr. | Militaer Kommandantur (Military Headquarters) |
| Mil.Verw. | Militaerverwaltung (Military Administration) |
| mit | with |
| Mitte | Center or Central |
| mot | Motorized |
| neu | new |
| neuen | new |
| Nord | North |
| Nordost | Northeast |
| Nordwest | Northwest |
| Norwegen | Norway |
| Nuernberg | Nuremberg |
| O.F.K. | Oberfeldkommandantur (Military Government Area Headquarters) |
| O.K. | Ortskommandantur (Garrison Headquarters) |
| Ob. | Oberbefehlshaber (Commander) |
| Oberfeldwebel | Master Sergeant |
| Obergefreiter | Lance Corporal |
| Oberkommando | High Command |
| Oberleutnant | First Lieutenant |
| Oberst | Colonel |
| Oberstleutnant | Lieutenant Colonel |
| Obkdo. | Oberkommando (High Command) |
| Ost | East |
| Ostkp. | Ostkompanie (Eastern Company -tactical group composed primarily of Soviets serving in the German Army). |
| Ostpr. | Ostpreussen (East Prussia) |
| Panzer | Armor |
| Polen | Poland |
| Polizei | Police |
| Pz. | Panzer (Armor) |
| Reich | Empire |
| Res. | Reserve |
| Res.Div. | Reserve Division |
| Res.Kps. | Reserve Korps (Reserve Corps) |
| Rheinbrueckenkdtr. | Rheinbrueckenkommandantur (Rhein Bridge Commander) |
| Ringkragen | Duty Gorget |
| Russ. | Russian - Soviet |
| Russland | Russia - Soviet Union |
| Sardinien | Sardinia |
| Schlesien | Silesia |
| Schuetze | Private |
| Sich. | Sicherheits (Security) |
| Sicherheits | Security |
| Sizilien | Sicily |
| Ski. | Ski - Snowshoe |
| Soldbuch | Identity Document/Pay Book |
| Span. | Spanish |

| | |
|---|---|
| SS | Schutzstaffeln (Protection echelon) |
| Stab | Staff |
| Stabsfeldwebel | Sergeant Major |
| Staffel | Echelon |
| Sturm | Storm |
| Sturmbrigade | Assault Brigade |
| Sturmdivision | Assault Division |
| Sued | South |
| Suedgriechenland | Southern Greece |
| Suedost | Southeast |
| Suedwest | Southwest |
| Tarnsoldbuch | False Identity Document |
| tmot | Partially otorized |
| Tropen | Tropical |
| Tross | Train (as in Baggage Train) |
| Trupp | Troop |
| Turk. | Turkish |
| u. | und (and) |
| Unteroffizier | Corporal |
| Ung.Div. | Ungarn Division (Hungarian Division) |
| Vo. | Volks (Peoples) |
| Volks | Peoples |
| Volkssturm | People's Army (last ditch troops) |
| W.E.K. | Wehrersatz Kommando (Recruiting Command) |
| W.K. | Wehrkreis (Military Area -Service Command) |
| W.K. Kdt. | Wehrkreis Kommandant (Military Area Commanding Officer) |
| Warschau | Warsaw |
| Wehr.Ers.Kdo. | Wehr Ersatz Kommando (Recruiting Command) |
| Wehrkreis | Military Service Command |
| Wehrmacht | Armed Forces |
| Wehrm.Befh. | Wehrmacht Befehlshaber (Armed Forces Commander) |
| Wehrm.Ortskdtr. | Wehrmacht Ortskommandantur (Armed Forces Garrison Headquarters) |
| Westungarn | Western Hungary |
| Wien | Vienna |
| z.b.V. | zur besonderen Verwendung (For special purposes) |
| z.V. | zur Verfuegung (at disposal) |
| Zugwach | Railroad Security |

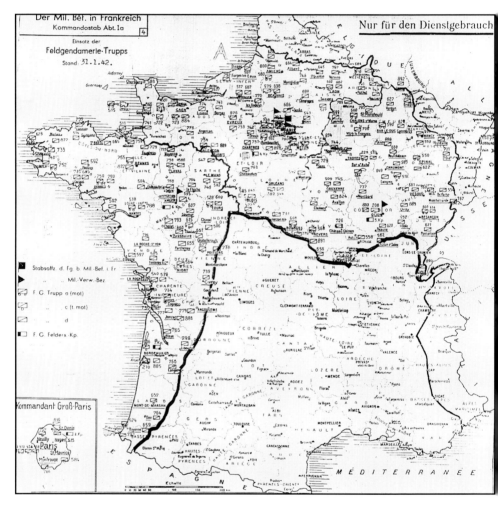

Official military map of Feldgendarmerie detachments assigned to occupied France, 31 January 1942.

124